Dedicated to the memory of
David Treffry of Place
for his constant friendship.

TREGONISSEY
to TRENARREN.

The Cornish Years
of A. L. Rowse

Valerie Jacob

5 Cannis Road
St. Austell

Preface

I confess that, though I had heard of A.L. Rowse since my schooldays and had read A Cornish Childhood in my early teens, I knew very little about the life of the great St. Austell historian. During his later years, however, whilst he was resident at Trenarren, I was able to meet and talk with him, share excursions around the Cornish countryside and eventually came to live alongside Dr. Rowse at Trenarren House in his last two years.

It was an honour to be there and look after him, a unique time to share and witness the results of his scholarship, wit and commanding presence. He had an unforgettable voice, often touching a high treble, but also warm and clear. One was compelled to listen.

This is an attempt to portray the Cornish years of Dr. Rowse's life and an account of my times with him. Others can quote, they can judge and analyse but in this personal tribute I hope to add that final touch to the man, the genius and true friend.

Acknowledgements

I am grateful to all Dr. Rowse's friends and admirers who have encouraged me to write this account of his life in Cornwall and my experiences at Trenarren. Realising that I had been fortunate to have had such a unique experience having been so closely involved with the household at Trenarren House, I resolved to consider it. Hopefully in some small measure I have done justice to this work and the life of Dr. Rowse.

My sincere thanks to Raleigh Trevelyan as literary executor, for permission to quote from Dr. Rowse's own poetry and books, notably A Cornish Childhood. Jack Blake helped me with many early recollections and details related to me by the late Phyllis Cundy, housekeeper to Dr. Rowse for twenty years, and Jack Gill. I also wish to thank Walter Thomas, retired to Brixham, who shared with me the All Souls chef's book for 1935.

Special thanks to my friend, Carol Folley, for transcribing my manuscript onto computer with such expertise.

I am most grateful to Dr. John Rowe who read the proof copy.

Lastly, but certainly not least, a big thank-you to my husband, Brian, for his unerring support and encouragement throughout my commitment.

5 Cannis Road   Valerie Jacob
St. Austell   2001

TREGONISSEY TO TRENARREN

A. L. Rowse

The Cornish Years

First published 2001 by Valerie Jacob
5 Cannis Rd, St. Austell
Copyright 2001 ©Valerie Jacob

ISBN
0-954 1505-0-3

Printed by Swift Print, St. Austell. 01726 70700

CONTENTS

Chapter One

TREGONISSEY VILLAGE AND FAMILY

The birthplace and early home of Alfred Leslie Rowse was in the small village of Tregonissey, on the outskirts of St. Austell in mid-Cornwall. The road along which the village had developed led northwards out of the town to the clay areas of Carclaze, Penwithick and Bugle. Tregonissey itself was a straggle of cob-walled cottages on the left-hand side of the road coming up from the town, with a farm at one end of the village, and the road lined with elms bordering fields on the right.

Almost in the centre of this small village was the Rowse enclave. William and Fanny Rowse, grandparents of A.L.Rowse, lived in a cottage (part of a smallholding) alongside the road. William augmented this income by working at Appletree Mine, on the cliffs near Charlestown. Two other cottages alongside the grandparents' home had been converted, by George and Kate Rowe, into living accommodation, a china shop and a little grocery shop. It was this latter shop which Richard and Annie Rowse, A.L's parents, took over and rented from Uncle George. Annie Rowse managed the shop, while Richard went to work in the clay pits nearby.

The village, so vividly described in *A Cornish Childhood* by A.L. was typical of many in Cornwall during the years leading up to the First World War, when family, friends and neighbours lived in a close community. In the best known photograph of the village taken about 1910, the young Leslie Rowse is seen standing on the pavement nearest the gabled porch, aged about seven or eight years, his elder brother George alongside. The photograph shows the square-fronted, slightly bowed window halfway along which was Uncle Rowe's china shop. The shop was comprised of two old premises, the larger display window for his chinaware, some of

The Tregonissey of Leslie Rowse's childhood. He is standing nearest the centre porch aged 7-8 years

which had "A present from Tregonissey" painted on the side. Alongside was the grocer's shop showing a rather high porch and a lot of roof projecting over the pavement. Leslie's parents succeeded to this shop after the retirement of Uncle and Auntie Rowe, having lived formerly, since their marriage in 1893, in Grandmother Rowse's old home.

The grocery shop premises had been converted in the 1860's from a former dame school in the little cottage, which Richard Rowse had attended as a boy. From there he went to another dame school at Polkyth and then the National School at Mount Charles. He often took dinner to his father at Wheal Eliza, nearby

Richard Rowse as a young man in Johannesburg. S. Africa.

at Boscundle, who related to his son in later years that he had been the first

2

person to test the telephone system, from the bottom of Wheal Eliza to ground level, and was directed to sing because he had a particularly fine voice. When he left Mount Charles School, Richard Rowse accompanied Uncle Rowe on his rounds (for a while) in the neighbouring villages selling china and collecting rags. Later, as a young man, he was persuaded to join his brother Bill, who was mining in South Africa, but he never settled and returned home after only three months there.

Elizabeth and Edward Vanson. A.L. Rowse's maternal grandparents.

Leslie's maternal grandparents lived in the Lodge for Tregrehan House along the St. Austell to St. Blazey road. Edward Vanson had been brought up at Quintrell farm near Crinnis whilst his wife Elizabeth had spent her early life on a farm in the parish of Duloe. She came to live with an aunt at Tywardreath after her father re-married and it was here that Edward met her, the Vanson's being a well-established family in Tywardreath.

After their marriage, Edward and Elizabeth settled at Quintrell farm, spending most of their life there until farm work and advancing years made a move necessary. From the farm the promotion to the Lodge, built in 1852 at Tregrehan,, was considered a great advancement by the old couple. Leslie enjoyed visiting them with his mother when the shop at Tregonissey was shut on Thursday afternoons, driving the two or more miles in the donkey and jingle. The young boy wandered in the grounds and in his later descriptions of these and the House, he claimed, "They opened up a window in my imagination as a boy".

3

Annie Vanson. A.L. Rowse's mother
Housemaid at Tregrehan House
1884 - 1889

There had formerly been another link with the Rowse and the Carlyon family who had lived continuously at Tregrehan since 1565 developing their property and family fortunes. Built on the southern slopes amidst fine parkland, the house employed many servants and outdoor staff. Whilst her parents were still farming at Quintrell, Annie Vanson had her first taste of employment as a young servant girl, from the age of fifteen to twenty years old, at Tregrehan House in the 1880s. Her next situation as housemaid was spent in service for the St. Aubyn family at St. Michael's Mount and from there to Dr. Stephen's house in High Cross Street, St. Austell. It was here that she met Richard Rowse who was a groom there for the town doctor. After their marriage at Charlestown Church in February 1893, they made their first home in Granny Rowse's cottage, who had died the previous October. The first child Hilda was born there, followed by George five years later but by the time Leslie was born in 1903, the family had moved into the shop premises.

During Leslie's early years, Hilda aged ten played a prominent role in tending and caring for him. Mrs. Rowse's main concern was the shop, open many hours each day, normal in Cornish villages in that era. In his autobiography, *A Cornish Childhood,* A.L. expresses his early dislike of the shop with its constant demands and routine. His help was expected and commandeered in the household. The young boy was expected to feed the "fowls" and the donkey, then take it to the field. He would have been asked to bring in the coal, fetch the milk from the farm, to chop sticks, draw a pint of lamp oil or weigh maize, thus helping to "mind the shop". As he grew older, all these menial jobs became heartily disliked as they interfered with the hours of reading that had become increasingly important to him.

Family outings were highlights in Leslie's life as they were so rare. There was a very special Sunday evening one, recorded in his poem, *"St. Mewan*

Church Bells", when the whole family were walking through nearby fields gathering bluebells which carpeted the way and the "silvery sound" of the neighbouring church bells were heard in the still evening air.

"It was the one time I remember when all the family moved as one."

1905-1906 Aged 2-3 years   *Young Leslie Rowse with his mother.*

Picnics at Porthpean were highlights of summer days when the Rowse children walked to Porthpean beach in the morning, the parents brought pasties for lunch, and the whole day was spent enjoying sand, shingle and sea. Porthpean has always been the favourite beach of St. Austell people. The young Leslie remembered the long walk home, uphill all the way to Tregonissey, the warmth of the sun on his shoulders and the tingling on the soles of his feet from the shingly sand as he lay in bed that evening. As he grew older and reading became more and more important in his life, Leslie recalled one of his favourite places of refuge in the fields opposite his home. Surrounded by lofty elm trees were ancient banks and an old cattle shed. Calling the place "Lost House", he found a haven of peace amongst the leafy quiet. The name Lostwood Road remained in the area after the Council houses were built on the fields.

The visual beauty of the world made an early impact. Expected to help in the household, the young boy was often abstracted by awareness of the beauty of Nature. In *A Cornish Childhood,* he recalls, "The purity of blue sky seen through the white clusters of apple-blossom in spring", one morning early on his way to school. He was awe-struck and claimed that he wondered about the perfection and the fragility of human life. On another occasion, he remembered that he, "spent considerable time in the garden gazing at two spiders' webs, absolutely beautiful, miracles of grace and architecture. The mist and rain had left tiny pearl drops, along each line of gossamer, the webs glistened as if bespattered with minute pearls and diamond drops. I watched them for several minutes." In later years in a poem entitled, *"Listening to Handel's Messiah"*, after the line "And the glory of the Lord shall be revealed", he remembered the primroses of childhood in the Pentewan Valley and the fields of Pondhu.

A very precocious child, who thought, read, wondered and reflected on life, set him apart at an early age. Instilled in his memory was the apple orchard in spring at Tregonissey, taking Neddy the donkey by starlight to be shod, reading and dreaming about South America on the Ledra at Trenarren, praying in St. Austell church on summer evenings during the First World War and seeing stars through the trees, which became the title of his first published poem while he was a pupil at St. Austell County School.

STARS, SEEN THROUGH THE TREES

The full moon, floating high in the frost-blue sky,
Bathes the world in a sea of shimmering light,
Whose haunting splendour, gleaming ghostly white,
Forbids the rest of Sleep, howe'er I try
To woo her to my pillows. So I lie
Dreamily watching the all-wondrous night:
The leafless trees' dusk network is alight,
Encrusted by the star-jewels, which defy
E'en the day of moonlight. Every star
Centres a frame of branch-threads intertwined.

It is gleaned from A Cornish Childhood that the young Leslie Rowse was secure in the family situation. Surrounded by family and friends, his life was further enriched by characters in the village who were willing to spend some time with the young inquisitive boy. Sensitive by nature, he responded to the people who would listen and answer his questions. He was an avid reader from a very early age, often preferring this pastime to that of joining the village children at their games in the street. Any pocket money he received was spent at the second-hand bookstall in the Market House in St. Austell where he later became a regular customer. He once earned enough money to buy an encyclopaedia by digging a bed of potatoes for his father.

A.L.Rowse lived in Tregonissey until 1922 when his parents gave up the shop and moved to a Council house at 24, Robartes Place. At nineteen years of age he began his life at Oxford.

Tregonissey, St. AUSTELL,

191

Bill-head and Tregonissey shop where
A.L. Rowse was born,
later altered and heightened

Bought of **R. ROWSE,**

GROCER AND TEA DEALER.

7

Chapter Two

SCHOOLDAYS

CARCLAZE ELEMENTARY AND
ST. AUSTELL COUNTY SCHOOL

Leslie Rowse was still only three years old when his sister Hilda took him up the hill from Tregonissey to the Elementary School at Carclaze. Apparently his mother had sent word to the headmaster that if he would not take her son on the role, she would have to keep Hilda at home to look after him. From the babies' class in the Infants' School, where toys and games were directed towards learning, Leslie soon progressed to the second class where arithmetic and reading were taught.

Carclaze class photo 1908
A.L. Rowse standing in the second row on extreme right in front of teacher

A. L. Rowse at
Elementary School aged 6-7 years

In an early class photograph aged four, A.L. later wrote on the back of it, "Small boy, sulking on extreme right, didn't want to be photographed, had to be dragged in last, finger stuck out in protest." Another photograph, taken at the Elementary School, when he was six or seven years old, shows a rather more amiable countenance. He loved school from the very beginning. The interest, books and learning that were available just suited his insatiable appetite for learning. He would often call at his aunt's house, Hillside, on his way home from school to bury his head in the books there, particularly the history section.

Leslie Rowse progressed rapidly from Standard to Standard. With his ability and aptitude for reading and learning, he soon passed through the Infant classes and subsequent Standards to that of the headmaster, Mr. H.I. Hugh, where his exceptional abilities were recognised. An infant teacher, Bessie Clemo, retained one of his workbooks containing exercises and essays of great merit for so young a mind. Thirty years later in *A Cornish Childhood,* the author pays tribute to this early teacher. He continued to correspond with her after receiving the workbook, which she had forwarded to him. She had followed his career throughout, from her house in King's Avenue, St. Austell and later from residential care at Caprera. From the headmaster's class, Leslie Rowse, aged eleven years was entered for a scholarship to the County School at Poltair. He was successful and so left Carclaze School at the end of the summer term to begin his secondary education in September 1915.

The new County School, which had been built in 1906-7 on a site ascending Tregonissey Road, facing south overlooking sloping fields towards St. Austell Bay, was a fine granite structure. Built at a cost of £6000, it could take 120 boys and girls, many paid for by their parents along with the scholarship holders. Opening in the winter term of 1908, with many of the pupils who had come from the old Pupil Teacher Centre at West Hill, its first headmaster was William Downing Raynor. An article in the copy of the first County School Magazine of the Winter Term 1908 provides an eye-witness account by "An old Girl," transferred from the West Hill Centre to the new school at Tregonissey Road. The "amazing spectacle" of this new building with a sanded carriage drive for bicycles was soon over-shadowed by the fine interior. The entrance lobby, with the *"looking glass,* the news of which spread almost as rapidly as the news of 'fire' does in St. Austell," led on through glass panelled doors to the wide corridors beyond. The masters in their black gowns awaited the new pupils and after prayers, directed them to appropriate classes and work began. The magnificent staircase with its wooden balustrades, corridors leading to classrooms overlooking St. Austell Bay, all must have seemed very grand. The building had a granite frontage, with carved coats of arms of both Cornwall and St. Austell above the central plinth and was surmounted by a dome.

County School St. Austell 1906 -07

Beginning in September 1915, under the headmastership of Harry Livingstone Lodge, Alfred Leslie Rowse began a new era with secondary education. The County School was even nearer to his home in Tregonissey than the previous one, and was just on the crest of the hill above St. Austell. He related in his autobiography that he was greatly impressed by the building, the number of different teachers for each subject, and the challenge of learning a foreign language, French. At the County School he could question, challenge an opinion and satisfy his curiosity. There were now over two hundred pupils at the school, with boys and girls fairly equal in number.

On entry, Leslie was placed in Form II, moved into Form III at the end of his first term and because he took first place in the form examinations at Easter was moved again to Form IV. Here he completed his first year holding a position of seventh out of twenty-seven pupils who on average were more than two years his senior. He excelled in History, English, Latin and French throughout his school life in classes with pupils always more than two years ahead in age, until he reached the Sixth Form. Headmaster's comments on the school reports were always "excellent" and "very promising". Added to this success and achievement at school, Leslie joined the choir of the Parish Church. He was a choir member from 1914 - 1920, becoming solo and head chorister and eventually when his voice broke, an alto member with the men. He enjoyed choir practices and church services combined with choir festivals and summer outings all providing social interest and musical education. In 1919, the Parish Church choir outing was to Bude, and Leslie then aged fifteen years accompanied the party of thirty men and boys.

The Choirboy aged 11 -12 years at St. Austell Parish Church

St. Austell 1919 Parish Church Choir Outing to Bude.
A.L. Rowse in school cap,on back row third from left.   Courtesy of E. Sandrey

In September 1919 when Leslie began his Sixth Form studies, the Headmaster was A. Godfrey Jenkinson, an Oxford graduate, who had returned to St. Austell after service in the First World War. At the end of this year the headmaster recorded, "Entirely satisfactory. I have great hopes for his future. He must at all costs have a good university career." Leslie's main strength in the subjects already mentioned, combined with Mathematics were his subjects for matriculation. These were noted as "special subjects" entering his Sixth Form career. The head acknowledged Leslie's work as a prefect and school librarian and commented on several reports of his conscientious service to the school.

Reading became the theme of Leslie's life. He read widely for several hours each day rarely deviating from his stringent timetable. However, he still enjoyed long walks around the countryside, nearly always with a book under his arm, complimenting stops to admire views. In his late adolescence he began to write poetry, encouraged by Mr. Jenkinson who submitted the poems to an anthology "Public School Verse", where two were chosen alongside those of scholars from the famous Public Schools.

The autumn edition of the school magazine 1916 recorded that Rowse was the librarian. He had only been at the school two years. By 1918 he became a prefect, co-editor of the magazine as well as the school librarian, all of which he continued to be until he left. In the Senior Local Examination that year, the magazine reported his success of a distinction in History. In the same edition, A.Leslie Rowse signed the Debating Society's report as Hon. Sec. and indicated the future success of the Society. The Literary Society's account of "Shakespeare and Music" followed with A. Leslie Rowse as its appointed secretary. During the evening meeting of this Society he had sung "Full Fathom Five" and "O Mistress Mine". The Literary Society presented two leather bound volumes of Kipling to a teacher, Mary Blank, who had been the founder of the Literary Society at the school. Miss Blank was leaving the school after five years to travel as a missionary in India. She had been Leslie's English teacher since he began at the County School and as secretary he made the presentation to her. Another contribution in that same magazine was "Luxulyan - Its Valley and Church" by Leslie Rowse.

During the period of the First World War many more women teachers came to the school. That Leslie Rowse responded to their sympathetic, intuitive approach is evident. His History teacher throughout most of his school life was R.M.Lewis. Inside a copy of R.L.Stephenson's "Travels With a Donkey", Miss Lewis wrote, "A.L.Rowse with grateful recollections of our journeyings - June 1920." Some years later Leslie had added, "Poor old schoolmistress had broken her ankle. I drove her to school in my donkey cart every day, rather reluctantly, afraid of ridicule." The schoolteacher he greatly admired was his English teacher Mary Blank. On the back of a 1919 Tewington House photograph, of which he and Miss Blank were members, Leslie had written in later years, "Nice Mary Blank."

Tewington House St. Austell County School. A.L. Rowse 4th from left on back row. Teachers Mary Blank and Gladys Medland

The magazine of the Spring Term 1920 recalled that Leslie Rowse had won a second prize of £4.0.0 offered by the navy League for an essay entitled, "The Difference between Sea Power and Militarism" which was open to all Secondary and County Schools in the British Isles. That year he also achieved First Class Honours and Distinction in English at the Senior Oxford examinations aged seventeen years. A school performance of Shakespeare's "As You Like It" was given after Speech Day in December 1919. The report noted a fine performance of Leslie's interpretation of Jacques. At Christmas 1920 a production of "Twelfth Night" was staged at the School's Speech Day. The character of Malvolio was played by Leslie, who excelled on stage, enjoying the experience of becoming a Shakespearean character. A younger pupil at that time,

Doris Julyan, recalled his compelling performance with great clarity only a few years ago. In his autobiography, Leslie attributed his success to the fact that he felt the pathos of Malvolio's character and empathised.

1920 County School Performance of Shakespeare's Twelfth Night.
A.L. Rowse, centre back as Malvolio. Noreen Sweet, centre seated as Countess Olivia.

The school magazine became an outlet for Leslie's literary essays. One article, "An Evening With A Book", featured Leslie's choice, "Lettres de Mon Moulin" by Daudet. He had taken the book up the hill to read at Carn Grey, comparing the scene before him to Corsica as featured in that book. The solitude and atmosphere of Carn Grey, Leslie's favourite haunt, appealed to him throughout his whole life.

Things I Love

Morning song of birds
Fresh recurring breath of dawning day
Scent of clover, new mown hay
Call of ploughman
Drowsy hum of bees.
Hail bashing the window pane
Light of fire on hearth
Bracken, wood fires, ivies and clinging mosses
Flecks of foam and spray the mill wheel tosses
The frugal wayside meal, cool spring water
Homecoming lit by the moon's low-hung lamp.

The different world of education already becoming more obvious to his family separated Leslie from his parents more and more as the years progressed. His mother's reply after a poem was read to her was, "Gid along. Taakin' op all that time to write a few 'ole verses." As a university career became important the headmaster suggested that Leslie should apply for a scholarship to Exeter College, Oxford favoured by many young men of West Country association. So a fevered spell of more reading was undertaken. One day Leslie remarked, "At school I do nothing but read. At home I do nothing but read, and have read seven books in the last few days." The forthcoming visit to Oxford to sit the examinations required by Exeter College became the mainspring of his thoughts and aspirations. He only had one month to prepare for this scholarship. Once again the demands of the shop irritated. This time his father grumbled because Leslie had neglected to ask the baker for the price of flour. "I don't care a scrap for these details, which keeping a half penny shop entails. I hate the shop," was later written in *A Cornish Childhood*.

During the Spring of 1921, Leslie had his first glimpse of Oxford as he sat for the scholarship at Exeter College. He reported later that he could not concentrate on the essay title. As he sat in Exeter College Hall, he had gazed in wonder at the stained glass, portraits and carved wood that surrounded him. He enjoyed the Latin and French papers and the English Literature one the most. While in Oxford he visited Christ Church Cathedral and hunted among the shelves in Blackwell's bookshop. It was his first visit to a city that began a lifetime appreciation of its colleges, halls, libraries, chapels and learning. After four days there, Leslie returned home and found a welcome release in playing hockey on the school field all Saturday afternoon. It appeared that players were in short supply, Leslie recruited four more to make a team. "They were only spectators at the football in the next field."

Leslie was not successful in gaining a scholarship at Exeter College but as he was only just over seventeen years old, the headmaster commented on the report for that term, "He need not be despondent on not securing a scholarship at the first attempt." The following year in 1922, another scholarship was suggested for Christ Church. The necessity for winning this one became of paramount importance in Leslie's mind. He wrote in his diary, "I have to get a scholarship to get away from the deadening atmosphere, mother washing clothes, father fiddling about with donkey, fowls, flour, logs, garden, stables and so on." He continued, "I must get to college somehow."

Messrs. Saunders, Parsons, Martin, Lodge, Richardson, Baker.
Misses Rich, Parry, Bond, Mr. Barritt, Misses Lewis, & Scales.
[Head Master]

County School Staff 1920 - 1921

During that year, his headmaster A.G. Jenkinson had left St. Austell to take up a post as head of Hemsworth Grammar School, Yorkshire but not before outlining plans for Leslie's future to include a County scholarship. Leslie sat for this in Truro and was successful. It was the first time that anyone at the County School, St. Austell had won the only scholarship available for the whole of Cornwall. The new headmaster, A.J. Barritt, a Cambridge graduate, having been handed over Leslie Rowse as "a special legacy", planned for an English scholarship at Christ Church. He made a "kindly impression" on the sixth form student and arranged for his pupil to meet Sir Arthur Quiller-Couch, head of the Cornwall Education Committee. Leslie was greatly honoured to meet the eminent Cornish literary character and was further encouraged. In the early summer of 1922, he once again visited Oxford to sit examinations. Here again, as at Exeter College, he was impressed and awed by the grandeur of Christ Church Hall, its portraits, splendour of the room, and the air of opulence. A week of examinations and interviews followed.

In his autobiography, Leslie recorded that the news of his success was first seen in the newspaper. He had gained a Christ Church scholarship. His school celebrated with a whole day's holiday and heartiest congratulations included those telegraphed from Mr. Jenkinson to his former pupil. He also wrote that he had been delighted to hear of the success and only regretted that he had not had the pleasure of announcing it to the school.

16

"Now for Oxford," he had written, indicating the next step. In May, another letter followed, in which he wrote, "For once I proved a true prophet and I feel that my life has not been in vain. I cannot be too thankful that I persuaded you to go up and try again. You have done splendidly and I am sure that if you make the most of your opportunities at Oxford, your future career will be fruitful of high achievement."

Owen J. Fogarty, who had tutored Leslie in English in the Sixth Form for two years, also wrote on hearing the news. In his letter he wrote, "Good news of Christ Church, the gates are opened. Have you read Tom Brown at Oxford? Your success has given me a joy that one experiences all too rarely. May it open to you all that your inner self yearns for."

The County and Oxford scholarships needed a further financial boost and so another interview was arranged with one of the City of London liveried companies. Leslie Rowse with his father made a first visit to London when he appeared before the Drapers' Company Board for a scholarship. He was successful and thus accumulated the two hundred pounds a year with which he thought he could manage at Oxford. A further fifteen pounds as year was provided by various literary and Cornwall Education Committee friends.

The summer of 1922 was spent enjoying Cornish walks, reading and preparing for the Oxford term in October, while Leslie's parents prepared to leave the shop premises to move to a new council house being built on the fields below Tregonissey. Leslie went to Helston to visit R.G. Rows a former Chairman of the Education Committee, accompanied by F.R. Pascoe the County Secretary, with whom he made a lasting friendship. During this summer, Leslie tutored the son of W.B. Luke, a St. Austell businessman. He gave lessons in Latin and Arithmetic, which took place at the Dower House, St. Austell and received two guineas, extra money towards the expenses of the oncoming term as an undergraduate.

When the new term began at the County School, Mr. Barritt contacted Leslie to write a play for the next Speech Day. With Quiller-Couch's (Q) permission, Leslie adapted *Troy Town,* which was produced in the Public Rooms, St. Austell on December 19th and 20th 1922. Leslie was present at the last performance and recalled being led on the stage by "Q", after the final curtain.

Leslie Rowse's connections with his old school continued for many years. He paid frequent visits there when down from Oxford. The school was given a further half-day holiday when he won his All Souls Fellowship in 1925.

A former scholar, who was at the school in 1921, wrote many years later, "I remember marvelling at his cultured speech and intonation and the excitement of his getting his scholarships." In the late 1920s, another contemporary stressed that on Leslie's visits, the pupils showed great deference, "almost bowing", as he went by. The school magazines continued to report the progress of its most illustrious scholar throughout the next ten years. The building extension and improvements were also noted. In 1925, a new sports pavilion was built, by Mr. Hopkins the woodwork master, with help from the boys, on the sloping field at the back of the school building. During the summer of 1926, Leslie gave a Workers' Educational Association lecture at the County School, with tea being served afterwards outside the new Sports Pavilion.

St. Austell County School Tea after A.L. Rowse's first W.E.A. lecture in 1926

The following years of Oxford research, politics, American lectureships and travel made major inroads into Leslie's time. It was not until 1977 that he visited the school again, after an absence of more than fifty years, when he awarded the prizes at Speech Day and recollected his very happy time there at the school from 1915 to 1922.

Speech Day at Poltair School - 1977. A.L. Rowse aged 74 years holding the silver dish made and engraved at the school and presented to him that evening.

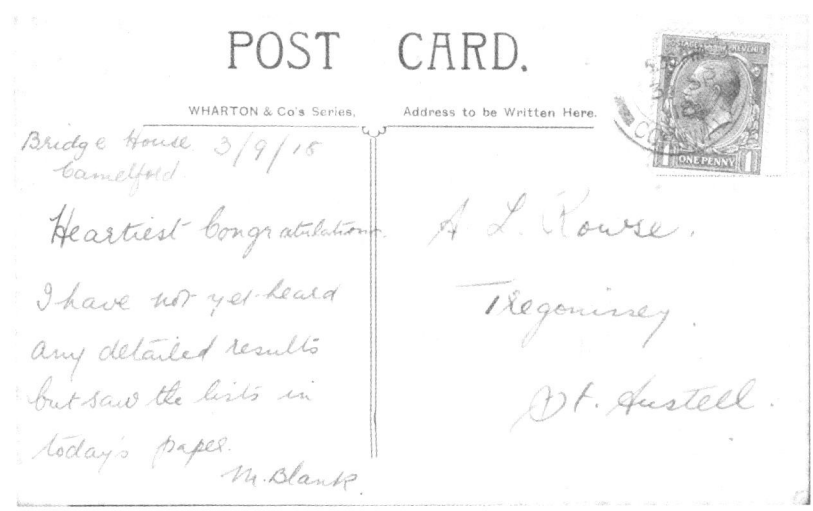

Chapter Three

OXFORD

CHRIST CHURCH 1922-1925

A move from the home at Tregonissey coincided with preparations that autumn with the first term of A.L. Rowse at Christ Church, Oxford. Table linen, crockery and cutlery were accumulated by his mother, now convinced, though scarcely reconciled to the fact, that her youngest child was set for a university career. Aunt Bessie presented her nephew with a silver napkin ring, on which his initials were engraved.

Christ Church Oxford Meadow Buildings. A.L. Rowse's room at extreme end - second floor up.
1922 - 1925

In early October 1922, A.L. left St. Austell station to travel to Oxford by train. On arrival there he made his way towards the grand college buildings of Christ Church. It must have been an emotive experience for the young Cornish scholar as he walked through the carved, vaulted entrance under Tom Tower with the vast expanse of Tom Quadrangle beyond. In later years he recalled his mixed feelings, but mostly of pride on entering Tom Gate.

The rooms allocated to him were in Meadows Buildings VI. He wrote home, "My rooms are my very own and beyond my wildest dreams. There is an enormous sitting room, twice the size of the front room at home. The windows look out over Christ Church meadows and the Walks."

The inventory and valuation of the sitting room furniture and the bedroom accoutrements amounted to £63.11.6 (£63.57). Weekly bills, called battels, for board and provisions showed how careful and abstemious the young scholar was. In one week the total bill from the Buttery, a refreshment room for the students was less than five shillings (25p) although coals and fagots to heat the rooms amounted to 6 shillings and 6 pence (32p). The kitchen bill for the same week's breakfasts was less than sixpence (5p) each day. Luncheon cost sixpence (5p) daily and evening dinner in Hall amounted to two shillings and six pence (12p). The kitchen total for that one week was £1.13.1 (£1.65) which when added to the gate and messenger dues of one shilling and sixpence (7p) the whole bill amounted to £2.6.0 (£2.30). As there were no luncheon dues at the weekend, one may assume that A.L. either dined out with friends, or went without. One week's food and heating bill was less than £2.50, more than a working man's weekly wage at home, but a very scanty sum for the average Oxford undergraduate from wealthy backgrounds.

Other expenses during that first term illustrate the frugal living adopted by the young Cornish undergraduate. For the whole term up to Christmas 1922:

Battels amounted to	£12. 2.2	(£12.11)
Room rent was	£ 7. 3.4	(£ 7.17)
Tuition fees were	£ 9. 0.0	(£ 9.00)
Window cleaning, chimney sweeping, carpet beating totalled	£ 1. 5.0	(£ 1.25)
Laundry	£ 1.11.2	(£ 1.56)
Electric light	£12.10.0.	(£12.50)
Hire of furniture	£ 1.12.0	(£ 1.60)

The total term's account was £47.16.7 (£47.83) thus depleting A.L's £200 per annum by the best part of a quarter, and therefore needing expenditure for books, clothes and travelling back to Cornwall to be considered carefully. Concern over money matters was constant during his student days.

A.L. recalled that the days of his first term at Oxford were the most crowded of his life and on the whole the happiest. The great theme was learning and literature versus history. He claimed that melancholy had gone and that he was more vigorous in mind. He hoped to retain the best of his old self for Cornwall and the best of his new self for Oxford.

Letters home contained anxious enquiries about his father who had been laid off along with others from Carclaze clayworks and as the shop had been relinquished there was no more income from that source. News of George, his brother, in Australia was not good as a poor harvest had been reported there and his sister Hilda's husband was not sure of work in California, so there was no one at home to help his parents financially. The juxtaposition of this world with A.L's Oxford environment is accentuated by the contents of a memorandum to undergraduates, October 1922. Special discipline and supervision of the type of company and places permitted to visit were listed. Entry was banned to bars, public houses, hotels, lounges and restaurants. Permission was needed to attend dinner in a hotel. The rules forbade attendance at public and private dances, public race meetings, pigeon shooting, coursing or any "scandalous or offensive game". The undergraduates were not allowed to keep or hire for more than one day a motor car or motor cycle of any kind without leave and on no account to take part in aviation! Open-air meetings of a political character were also forbidden along with processions or demonstrations likely to cause a disturbance of the peace, and no smoking while in Academic Dress! There was nothing amongst the rules that would have bothered A.L. Certainly entertainment was not part of his Oxford scene and his income would have automatically barred him from partaking in most of the pursuits mentioned. His sights were firmly fixed on books and learning to the exclusion of all else. A.L. returned home for Christmas 1922. He watched the performance of his own adaptation of *Troy Town* in the Public Rooms, St. Austell, in the presence of Sir Arthur Quiller-Couch.

During the vacation, he took long walks to Carn Grey, Crinnis and Luxulyan with friends, interspersed with visits to Tregrehan Lodge to see his grandmother. Throughout the time reading was still his passion and he begrudged Christmas Day and Boxing Day celebrations as there was no time for books on those dates. Despite this, A.L. enjoyed the closeness of the family life, referring fondly to his parents as "primitive and simple souls" and left for his second term at Oxford with some pangs of homesickness.

The Cornwall Education Committee were keenly monitoring the progress of A.L. Rowse. R.G. Rows, on behalf of the Education Committee expressed pleasure at the news from Oxford of the first term. "I am much pleased though not surprised to find that your first impressions of Oxford were delightful. For the first time in your life you have been living in the midst of traditions which are more exciting and ennobling than would be found possibly anywhere else, and these in my opinion stand first in importance as an educating and uplifting force. The shades of Oxford's great men who have lived for the past five hundred years press on you on every side." 3.1.1923, The Willows, Helston.

At the beginning of his second term at Oxford, A.L. wrote, "Heavenly place this is." Throughout his years there, he always loved the sound of the bells from the various colleges, the quadrangles, gardens and walks around college interiors into which he now had privileged access. Some of the views around the city reminded him of Cornwall, a suitable field for Neddy, a sunset or mists lying in the water meadows, a poetic vision of the beauty of Nature. In later years A.L. often wrote that his years at Oxford were the source of great happiness. The entry to Christ Church, its grandeur, architecture, Cathedral, Hall, splendid mediaeval kitchens and all the traditions, was his entry to a paradise. From the restricted background of working class village life A.L. wrote, "What I found was, that this was my nature."

In March 1923, A.L. was persuaded to change from English to History as a subject for his degree. This entailed a strenuous programme of new reading and tutorials, but he knew that the dons were right in the decision. "History provided a far better intellectual training and proper background for research." It was during this period however that ulcer symptoms developed and bouts of pain and sickness became a constant fear. Oxford was an enriching experience in every way. The tutors, libraries, the impressive buildings, Radcliffe Camera, Sheldonian, architecture of Halls, Chapels and buildings must have appeared awesome. A.L. encountered sons of the most privileged families whose own progression to Oxford was assured from birth. He maintained his individuality, enjoying company of his peers but at his own discretion and living carefully within his means.

While at Oxford, A.L. became an enthusiastic member of the Labour Movement and this became his main interest alongside his academic work. He fulfilled the post of secretary and later chairman of the University Labour Club. It followed a middle of the road policy supporting Clement Attlee and Ernest Bevin. In June 1923, Lloyd George paid a visit to the Oxford Union. In his *Cornishman at Oxford,* A.L. wrote, "Everywhere one met people of interest." He also claimed that the most important part of college life was not the formal lectures and tutorials but the constitutional discussions with ones contemporaries, the cleverest boys from the famous Public Schools. There was constant discussion and debate. Wystan Auden and David Cecil read some of A.L's early poetry. The mental excitement of becoming an officer of the Labour Club, a member of the Essay Club at Christ Church, writing his undergraduate papers, poetry, and keeping his diary as well as extensive reading constituted an exacting lifestyle.

By the end of his first year at Oxford, A.L. related that he had £17 with which to settle his bills and that he would have about £10 left to last until the following October when he would commence his second year. One advantage of the shortage of money, he claimed, was that he came home to Cornwall each vacation. Before the end of that first year, however, he applied to the college grant system and was given £10. This was allocated immediately as a contribution to the household expenses during the summer vacation of ten weeks.

Oxford undergraduate on vacation at 24 Robartes Place

Throughout this long vacation, A.L. continued his customary and beloved country walks, Carn Grey to Luxulyan and Porthpean to Trenarren. The County School Swimming Sports were held at Porthpean in July 1923. After the events, A.L. was invited for the first time by Mrs. Petherick, along with the school staff and governors, to tea at Porthpean House. Whilst there, he was introduced to Henrietta Treffry who invited him to Place, Fowey. During this visit, they discussed the Lewis Carroll

24

connection with Christ Church. Charles Lutwidge Dodgson (1832-1898), known later as Lewis Carroll, a mathematics don, with a passion for photography, had been a long term resident of Christ Church, from his undergraduate years when he arrived in Oxford in 1851 and, except for vacations, where he remained for the rest of his life. After a boat trip to Godstow with the Dean's children in the summer of 1862, he had written *Alice's Adventures in Wonderland,* inspired by Alice Liddell and her two sisters.

Many hours of reading for the History Schools were fitted into the vacation routine and six or seven hours a day were not unusual. At the end of July, a perforated appendix meant an operation at St. Austell Cottage Hospital and several weeks of recuperation. Financial worries at home, where the £100 nest egg from the shop at Tregonissey had dwindled to £40, were a cause for concern. An unexpected windfall of £15 from three benevolent friends of Quiller-Couch, plus an increase of £25 a year from the Education Committee, somewhat resolved the financial strain.

The second Oxford year introduced more reading, the secretaryship of the Labour Club meetings, research and writing poetry. Frugal living was still the norm but for the first time A.L. took another fellow student out to dinner. The bill came to 9 shillings (45p). He immediately regretted the extravagance, recording later that this sum would have purchased Trevelyan's *Age of Wycliffe,* which he now needed for his studies. Friendship with David Cecil, Richard Pares, Bruce McFarlane, Jack Simmons, and later with Adam von Trott and Norman Scarfe, were furthered in walks around Oxford, visits, evensong at the Cathedral, intertwined with tutorials and avid reading programmes. Plymouth born Mark Thomson, and F.L. Harris from Cornwall were entertained to lunch or tea.

Politics provided an interesting diversion for A.L. who, as secretary, arranged the meetings with current political speakers. It seems that his old headmaster, now at Hemsworth Grammar School, was concerned that the distraction might prove to be detrimental to A.L.'s career. In a letter to Oxford, A.G. Jenkinson advised A.L. to be wary of devoting too much time to Socialism and social problems. "I am most anxious that your literary career should be a creditable one and that you should get the very best out of your life at Oxford," he wrote. His advice to Leslie continued gently admonishing him about being too cynical of the Public Schools, reminding him of the Great War and the losses of young officers from those very schools. He reminded A.L. that the Public School boys were as critical of him as he was of them, and he also commented, "It does you good to rub shoulders with all and sundry. That is the advantage of Oxford."

Poetry, and the writing of his verse, was a release from other academic goals. He was invited to meet the great poet Robert Bridges (1834-1930) and Poet Laureate from1913-1930, at his beautiful home, Chiswell, on Boar's Hill. During the second year at Oxford, A.L. determined to enter a poem for the Newdigate Prize, a prestigious annual award. The prize money would make a holiday to Brittany possible and provide extra cash for his mother and father. He chose as a title, *The Life of the English poet Byron,* composed during his second Christmas vacation. It was submitted early in 1925 in his third and final year at Christ Church. He admitted that he was pleased with the poem although he had never written such a long one of three hundred lines before. The result, published just before A.L. sat his Finals, awarded him the "proxime accessit" (runner-up) for the Newdigate. He was very disappointed that he had not won. Some small consolation was that "Q", in his day, had also been in the same position.

In June 1925 A.L. took his final examinations at Christ Church. The Final Honour School of Modern History was composed of eleven papers of three hours each spread over six days, and further complemented by an oral examination in July. The results were announced before he returned to Cornwall. He had achieved a First along with fifteen others out of 270 candidates. Congratulations from Oxford dons and Cornish friends poured in after the Oxford results were published in *The Times.* It was a major triumph as it was well known that a History First was notoriously hard to achieve.

To this great honour was added the final accolade of being invited to apply for a Fellowship at All Souls College. There were two Prize Fellowships awarded each year to the two most promising students from the whole of the University colleges. Another letter of congratulations from his old headmaster at St. Austell County School followed the History First news. In it, A.G. Jenkinson mentions the All Souls Fellowship. "It would be a brilliant success if you got one as it is the highest ambition of an Oxford scholar and the crowning point of a successful academic career."

ALL SOULS COLLEGE, OXFORD

After his return to St. Austell, A.L. spent the long vacation reading, this time in preparation for the Prize Fellowship. All Souls College fronting The High in Oxford had no undergraduates. Half of the Fellows were academics and the rest represented public life in the Foreign Office, were diplomats, ambassadors, Cabinet ministers, Governors or church dignitaries. Applying for a Fellowship in September 1925 entailed more arduous examinations in history, politics, law and a "viva" or interview, as well as the ordeal of dining with the Warden and selected guests at High Table. Amongst the letters of congratulations on his History result was one from "Q" at Fowey including a gift of £15. A.L. was overjoyed at the thoughtfulness of his friend as with the money he was able to buy his first dinner suit, shirt, silk scarf and cashmere socks, the correct dress for dining at All Souls.

When the results were published, A.L. telegrammed at once and then wrote to his parents. He was overjoyed, he had won a place and always claimed that it was the happiest moment of his whole life. Mr. Barritt, headmaster at the County School gave the school a half-day holiday when the news reached him. The announcement heralded many more congratulatory letters. It was even more praiseworthy because A.L. was the youngest ever appointed as a Fellow and the first from a working class background.

Cornwall County Council, Truro City Council and St. Austell Urban Council reported how proud they were of his great achievement. The report in the *West Briton* newspaper termed Alfred Leslie Rowse as "the St. Austell clay worker's son in a meteoric rise through the academic world." At only twenty one years of age, he was labelled as, "A precocious curiosity, maturing to voracious intelligence alloyed with a determination that enabled him to win scholarships and battle his way to Oxford."

On November 6th 1925, A.L. entered his signature in the All Souls Register, following his election on All Souls Day, November 1st, when he had sat next to the Archbishop of York at the initiation service. He wrote to his parents, "I am amazed at my good fortune in becoming a Fellow. This college is the most

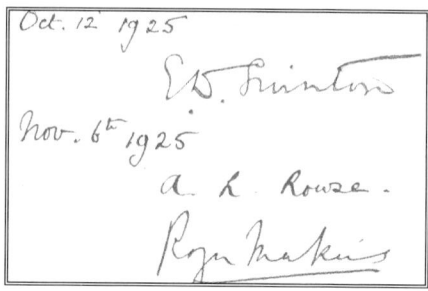

A.. L. Rowse's signature in the All Souls Admission Book

select in Oxford." He described the vast estates that the college helped to administer both in the country and town property. The Fellowship was worth £300 a year with extra money for teaching and examining. Living at All Souls meant moving into an upper class mode of life. A.L. wrote home that there was, "Dining by candlelight, the great candles in silver branched sconces." The irony of all this was not lost on him as he removed his belongings from Christ Church on a hand barrow through the Oxford streets. At All Souls he chose an upstairs set of rooms in the Old Quadrangle because they were airier and looked out on the lawn of the Warden's garden and were overlooked by the spire of St. Mary's Church.

A. L. Rowse's first set of rooms at All Souls 1925 - 1940

To these rooms, which he kept for fifteen to sixteen years, A.L. brought his furniture and books and as his financial position improved he searched Oxford shops for fine rugs, silverware and ornaments. Some of these early purchases

28

with their price tickets still underneath were in his home at Trenarren until his death. The John Wesley ornament, the Staffordshire Scots figures, papier mache letter racks and a Gothic shaped mirror were all collected in his early period at All Souls. In 1927, he purchased an Ibach piano from the County Music Stores, St. Austell, for despatch to Oxford.

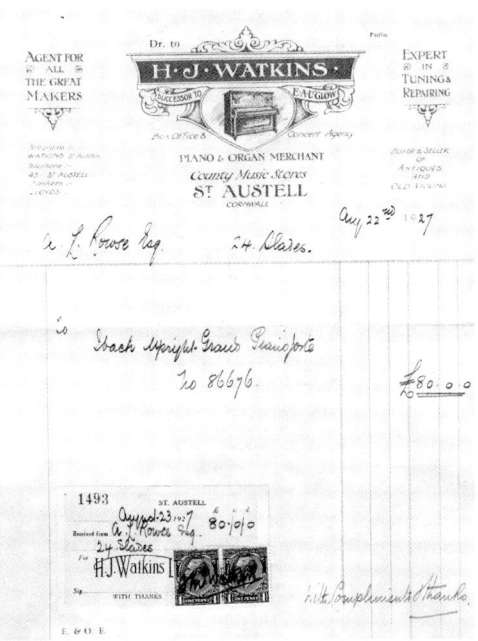

Piano Bill

In his diary of October 1925, A.L. noted, "Since I have settled in I have been recreating myself by talk and listening to talk, lunching and dining out and meeting all sorts of people, what a pleasant place this is ~ the pleasantest place on earth I suspect, but that's the danger."

Sir Charles Oman, making a kindly approach, mentioned the fine example of eighteenth century wallpaper which had once graced the dining room of the White Hart Hotel, St. Austell, formerly the town residence of Charles Rashleigh, a wealthy eighteenth century benefactor of nearby Charlestown who had built the harbour and inner basin there. A.L. regretted that he had never heard of it but determined to see the remaining panel on his next vacation. He recognised immediately the protected environment of All Souls, that it was here surrounded by the interesting, often brilliant conversation and delightful company that he had found his ideal refuge.

In early December, A.L. was invited to John Masefield's to tea when the aged poet and his wife made him feel welcome as the conversation was partly about Cornwall. Subsequently, he dined with John Buchan, a great experience. He noted, "What a rare opportunity, the unexpectedness of it took my breath away." Yet despite all this grandeur and gracious living, Cornwall was never far from his mind. News that Grandmother Vanson had died and that her husband was also very ill arrived at Oxford. He noted, "I think now of those golden evenings at Tregrehan, the pheasants strutting under the trees in the park and the light falling under the leaves and granny coming out in the cool to sit in the corner seat while grandfather dug up new potatoes or pottered about among the rose bushes." When he heard the evening bells of Magdalen college they reminded him of those in the parish church, St. Austell.

A.L's work at All Souls was purely intellectual. He was able to buy many more books for his research with the extra money from tutorials and teaching. The Codrington library at All Souls and the Bodleian library were a Mecca for an intellectual life. As well as research, he decided that the German and Italian languages were to be his next hurdle, augmented by travelling abroad, which he could now afford to contemplate. Part of his plan was for research, booklets on the Labour Movement, History, Literature and poems. He decided that all this would go towards a more enduring reputation than any drudgery, as a tutor, would achieve. He had decided to travel abroad to improve his health as symptoms of ulcer trouble were recurring regularly, then to return to research and writing. He wanted to publish. In his first term at All Souls he wrote a booklet entitled *On History* and was paid £15. For the first time, A.L. was in the position to send money home to his parents on a regular basis and this he continued to do until his mother moved out of the Council house at Robartes Place to the house he had purchased at Porthpean Road.

Highlights of the early years at All Souls were meeting Walter de la Mare and the Poet Laureate Robert Bridges. For the first time in his life he was able to return hospitality freely by offering lunch or dinner at All Souls. From a menu book still preserved by Mr. Walter Thomas, who was an apprentice chef at All Souls at this time, are records of lunches prepared for Mr. Rowse ~ lunch for 7 or 8:

Supreme Sole Laitance	3 - 6	17p
Poulet roti anglaise	15 - 8	78
Salade		
Flan de Pomme et Creme	3 - 6	17
	£1 - 3 - 2	£1 . 12

Mr Rowse Dinner for 3 at 7.15pm:

Consomme Friar Tuck	1 - 6	7p
Sole meuniere aux champignons	3 - 3	16
Cotellette d'agneau grille	4 - 0	20
Tartelette aux fruits Chantilly	1 - 6	7
	10 - 3	50p

During the Easter vacation of 1926, A.L. visited Paris, his first holiday abroad. He settled into a small pension in the Quarter amid the book stalls along the Seine. Here he was totally absorbed with history, buying books and volumes of music of Schumann, Schubert, Chopin, Mozart and Bach.

In the summer term he was invited to stand for the history donship now vacant at Christ Church. He was recommended by his old tutor and believed that an interview was merely protocol. The appointment of another applicant was quite bewildering. The decision stunned A.L., his pride was sorely wounded and he turned his back on his previous college. It was almost fifty years before he set foot in Christ Church again and that was to deliver the memorial address for his old tutor Keith Feiling.

Comforting himself that drudgery as a tutor was not his ideal, A.L. set his sights towards writing. It had already been suggested that a Study of the Reformation in Cornwall would be an ideal subject and eventually this came to fruition with the book, *Tudor Cornwall*.

Later in 1926, the ulcer and peritonitis flared again and an emergency operation followed in Oxford. Mr & Mrs Rowse were summoned from Cornwall but despite the

All Souls interior

seriousness, the danger passed. Quiet times at All Souls followed, winter tea-times around the fire where kindly talk and friendliness prevailed. In 1939, A.L. moved to another set of rooms within the college, behind the twin Hawksmoor towers and looking out on the Warden of New College's garden.

Teaching for the History School at Oxford augmented the All Souls income of £300 pr annum. A.L. added examining, lecturing for the W.E.A, and reviewing, as well as writing articles. His political thinking and politics were an important development running alongside that of a research programme. The involvement with the Labour Party at Oxford lasted throughout the 1930s. Historical research was extended to the Public Record Office in London and its first result was *Sir Richard Grenville of the Revenge*. This heralded a lifetime of interest in Elizabethan England and sixteenth century history, to which A.L. dedicated much of his life's work.

Life at All Souls was highlighted by the grand university occasions. The Encaenia procession through the Oxford streets and ensuing lunch each June encompassed a magnificent gathering of two hundred guests in the Codrington library. All heads of Oxford colleges were represented, political figures and grandees. At one luncheon party in 1945, General Eisenhower was the guest of honour along with Field Marshall Montgomery and Lord Alanbrooke.

Encaenia Procession 1966. A. L. Rowse at right hand corner.

32

First published in 1941, *Tudor Cornwall* was an impressive work of scholarship finalising the massive amount of Elizabethan research which took A.L. ten years to amass, and two years to write. A successor to this book was planned on the whole Elizabethan Age in all its aspects, a portrait of the whole society. Taking almost another ten years to complete, *The England of Elizabeth* was published in 1950, with a second volume to follow. A.L. confessed, "It takes everything I have in me to write a book like *The England of Elizabeth* or *Tudor Cornwall* and to write them satisfactorily I have to give up everything for them."

Another diversifying interlude developed about this time when the Warden Sumner, head of All Souls, died. As A.L. had held the post of sub-warden for some time, he was encouraged to stand as applicant for the Wardenship of the college where he had been a Fellow for twenty-six years. He had often encountered difficulties with the younger fellows who were not "working" or meriting their honorary place. A fierce contest resulted in the election of John Sparrow as the new Warden. A.L.'s great disappointment was once more veiled in relief that now his time could be devoted entirely to his own life. Writing later he mentioned, "I need the absolute concentration fenced off from outside to accomplish my work. I need to clear a space, a desert around me while I settle in the green and life-giving oasis of my own mind." It was a stroke of good fortune that about this time a decision to turn his back on England coincided with an offer from the Huntington Library in California for regular visits as a Research Associate. This library was founded to study the English Renaissance and combined both History and English Literature. It was an ideal situation. For several successive years, A.L. spent the winter in California, spring and autumn at All Souls and summer in Cornwall. This continued until 1974 when he retired from residence at the college where he had 'lived' for almost fifty years.

Two of A.L.'s books featured All Souls. In 1961, *All Souls and Appeasement* had been published explaining the politics and involvement of the college leading up to the Second World War. The second volume in 1993, *All Souls in My Time,* gives an account of events and personalities vividly remembered by the author at the age of ninety.

A.L.'s memories of All Souls were always a 'balm' in later years. His total recall of people, incidents and conversations lasted throughout his life. Ever generous with his Cornish friends, he invited them to Oxford to stay at All Souls. One of his staunch supporters and friend, Jack Gill, talked with awe of his stay there, the delight of A.L. as he showed him the college buildings and the tables set for dinner, polished silver on mahogany tables and the friendliness of the other Fellows. The conversation centred on Cornwall and Jack's work with the China Clay Company so that he felt at ease amongst such august company.

The memories of the happy life at All Souls are reflected in A.L.'s poetry. He always loved, "The bells of St. Mary's a regular accompaniment to dinner in Hall on Sundays," " The rose-flush of dawn on the Radcliffe Camera," " the great chestnuts of the Warden's garden, mountainous masses of green and white blossom in the tapestry time of the year." He recalled walks back to his rooms from the Codrington library when the twilight emphasised the twin Hawksmoor towers and watching, "The fantasy with which the half lights of winter clothed the grotesque and absurd in stone." Other memorable occasions were dining in Hall for the feast of All Souls' Night, a celebration of the foundation of the college, and the following All Souls' Day when the service in the chapel began with the Founder's Prayer.

In 1988 A.L. paid his last visit to Oxford and All Souls. He recalled sitting in the chapel there remembering his many former friends, and the freemasonry of the eminent old Fellows who met for All Souls' Day each year.

In the Common Room Garden - All Souls College July 1984

Chapter Four

POLITICS IN CORNWALL AND OXFORD

Linked with A.L.'s work at All Souls was the world of politics, predominantly with the Labour Party to which he adhered for over a decade. He had written addresses for the Labour Club in Oxford whilst still an undergraduate at Christ Church. Speeches and addresses from some of the leading Labour politicians of the day became an avid concern of the serious-minded A.L. Rowse. Stemming from his working-class background he had a real empathy for the Labour Movement in Britain.

By 1924 A.L. was Chairman of the Labour Club, inviting dons sympathetic to the Labour cause and Members of Parliament to speak at the meetings. At home in August that year he walked to Mevagissey to attend a Labour meeting there, as a supporter of the Welsh Labour speaker. It was in Oxford, however, during the decade 1930 - 1940 that A.L. became actively involved. Reinforced by his early book, *Politics and the Younger Generation*, was the theme of a better world for Britain after the First World War, and that the best hope lay in the common interest of the working classes.

In 1927 a speaker from the Unionist Association, touring St. Austell, stopped at the end of Robartes Avenue. A.L., at home on vacation, joined the gathered crowd to listen. Another Worker's Union meeting at Lane End, Tregonissey added to an already strong desire to represent the Labour Party in Cornwall as a Member of Parliament.

In his autobiography, *A Cornishman Abroad,* noting the years 1925 -29, A.L. quotes, "I don't think I should have been so much impelled into politics, if I hadn't become a Fellow of All Souls. Here the distinguishing mark of college life was public affairs." Therefore in 1929 he became a Labour candidate for Penryn and Falmouth, concerned about how things were going in Britain and emphasising his working-class background in his speeches.

In September 1929, the selection meeting at Truro chose A.L. Rowse as its candidate for Penryn and Falmouth where the main block of Labour voters were the dock workers. From this event a series of propaganda meetings were organised out in the clay mining regions surrounding St. Austell. The clay villages tended to vote Liberal, supporting their bosses in the clay mines. For many years, Cornwall had been entrenched in the Liberal Movement. A.L. saw the prime task for Labour in Cornwall was to bring home the futility of voting Liberal.

The busy intellectual life at All Souls was now interspersed with Labour meetings and fund raising in Truro and St. Austell. He had a team of friends, headed by Claude Berry, who supported his ideals at the political meetings during 1930. A.L. travelled around the clay and fishing villages, inland to St. Blazey, St. Stephens, Bugle, and even to Camborne. He claimed that from these occasions on the street corners he learned the art of making himself clear.

Returning to All Souls after the summer vacation, A.L. conferred with the Fellows. Warden Salter had considerable inside knowledge and influential friends among political figures and statesmen at the centre of British foreign affairs. At times life was overshadowed by politics and Hitler's threat to Europe. A Betting Book kept in the Smoking room at All Souls recorded wagers between the Fellows. A.L.'s careful bets with his contemporaries illustrate his serious political leanings.

January 9th 1933
"Hudson bets Rowse 2/6 (12p) that Trotsky will return to place in the U.S.S.R within one year from today." The settlement was paid by G.F. Hudson.

One year later the same Fellow placed the same sum with Rowse that the two Great Powers will be at war by Midsummer Day of that year. Leslie won that bet too. The world powers of Russia, Italy, Japan and Germany, with leaders Stalin, Mussolini, Emperor Hirohito and Hitler, were used by all contenders in the betting stakes.

In January 1931, A.L. was chairing meetings for the Labour Party with such notable speakers as Clement Attlee, Ernest Bevin and Herbert Morrison. Attlee gave unstintingly of his time, walking around the clay area with A.L. on campaigns, and the three gave many platform addresses for the aspiring political figure.

In the 1931 election he was not successful in gaining the constituency. His cause was hampered by the allegations of the other parties, the recurring trouble of his duodenal ulcer acerbated by intense mental concentration and combating rumours published in the local newspapers to discredit his cause.

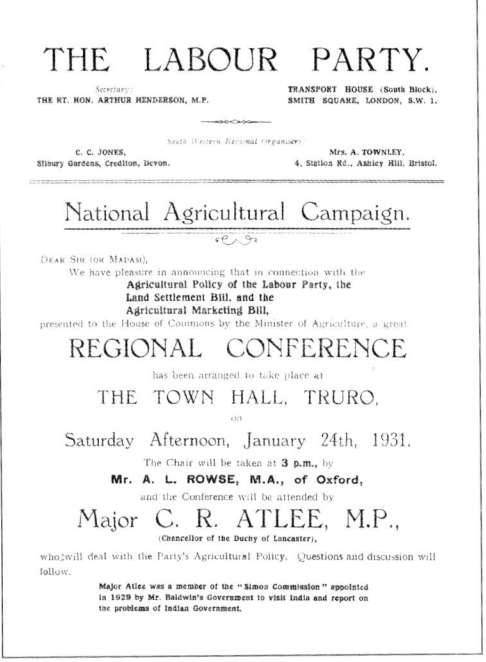

Labour Party Announcement

Throughout the following years, A.L. continued allegiance to the Labour Party and its work in Britain. Leading up to the next General Election, he campaigned in Cornwall throughout the summer months, combining this work with the University terms, which included an arduous lecture programme, examinations and history research in London for his next book. However, A.L.'s spirits were always buoyed up by thoughts of recuperating in Cornwall. In Oxford, he was often so tired and weary of work, longing to be home, and complained that he was nervy and often in the worst possible temper.

Sometime between the 1931 and 1935 elections, A.L. bought his first car, mainly so that he could be driven to the more remote parts of his constituency but also, with his brother George as driver and mother as passenger, he could visit places such as Trerice or Rialton, which he wished to explore in connection with his next planned book. The car was kept at Robartes so that Mrs. Rowse and her friends could be taken out for a drive and picnics when George could manage to take them.

A.L continued to stand as candidate for Labour in the next election of 1935, again for Penryn and Falmouth. In a leaflet, addressed to *Fellow Cornishmen and Women,* the issue of an Armaments Race and its dangers were revealed. The Labour Party pledged to carry on a peace policy begun in 1929 through the League of Nations. Appeals to the population included:

"As a Cornishman I am naturally concerned for Cornwall. What has been done for our depressed industries? What have the present Government done for the fisheries, for Cornish fishermen or for china-clay?"

The strong line was:

"Peace abroad and Social Progress at home."

A.L. Rowse
24 Robartes Place,
Slades,
St. Austell.

The result of the 1935 General Election was still a defeat for the Labour Party and A.L. as its parliamentary candidate for Penryn and Falmouth. This time, however, the Party held second place in this constituency and was pleased with the thirteen thousand votes obtained by their candidate.

As well as election speeches A.L. supported local events. In December 1937 a new Fire Station was built in St. Austell at the junction of Priory and Bodmin Road. A brand new fire engine had also been purchased at a cost of £1580. Leslie Rowse was approached by the Urban District council to officially open the new Fire Station. It was one of his first public duties in the local area.

Opening the new Fire Station. St. Austell in 1937

One of the most interesting aspects of A.L's political career was his link with the inauguration of a politically based newspaper, *Cornish Labour News* founded by Claude Berry. A.L. contributed articles to the paper, which was published monthly and cost one penny. In the May 1937 edition, he contributed, "Home thoughts from Abroad" including mention of Herbert Morrison and Ernest Bevin due to speak at a Demonstration in Camborne. There were references to Claude Berry, "The inspiration of this paper" and to Charles Henderson the great Cornish antiquarian scholar who had died in Italy in 1933 and was buried in the English cemetery in Rome. Scenes of Easter Sunday services in the parish church of St. Austell were evoked and of gathering primroses (with which to decorate the church) in the Pentewan Valley. He further claimed that he wished to be a spokesman for the Cornish people.

Throughout the whole of the decade 1930-1940, A.L. took an active part in the Labour Party. Term time was still for teaching, examining, researching, and lecturing at the Workers' Educational Association meetings in the evenings and Labour conferences. His research programme of the English sixteenth century meant that he had to live part time in London, for Public Record Office original manuscripts and the British Museum whilst lodging in Brunswick Square. In 1934, he accepted a lectureship for two days a week at the London School of Economics. Here he had contact with Harold Laski and R.H. Tawney, eminent economic historians, and the chance to lecture on the "History of Socialism in nineteenth century England" which was right in his line.

All this mental work, while actively involved in the political scene took its toll. Another operation in 1938, with a third in the early years of the war added to the stresses of an academic and political career.There were many anxious friends in Cornwall at this time. Mrs. Rowse received numbers of enquiries and kindly reassuring letters after her son's operation in 1938. Her friends wished that he would give up the idea of getting into Parliament. One added dryly, "When he does get there he will only be furious with them all and put a greater strain on himself." Later by 1943 after Leslie had left the active political scene, another friend wrote to him, "I am glad you have decided to give up politics and devote your time to writing and research. It will at least give you a period free from worry and political controversy."

It is clear that the ten years of political endeavour were frustrating to a man of A.L.'s temperament who because of his discussions and connections with some of the most able and far-thinking men of the day, advisers connected with government circles, could foresee and predict the outcome in Europe. A.L. felt he knew what was happening in world affairs and he was constantly driven to the point of despair about ineptitudes of which he faithfully tried to warn the public. In his last speech, in St. Austell, as a candidate for the Labour Party, A.L. expounded, "Every time you vote for Chamberlain and appeasement it is a nail in the coffin of your own sons." When Neville Chamberlain succeeded Stanley Baldwin as leader of a Conservative government in 1940, it proved that Leslie had correctly forecast the loss of thousands of lives in the war years.

The West Country Magazine edited in 1946 by J.C. Trewin includes an article entitled "Fighting an Election" by A.L. Rowse. The hustle and bustle, ceaseless comings and goings, excitements and agitations along with eloquent speeches, were not what were chiefly remembered. It was the Cornish countryside, buildings and villages, framed by hedges and woods, on the daily drives into Truro that he recalled. Describing them in eloquent terms marked with the sense of history incorporated in the place names with their meanings, the article is a masterpiece of literary description. By this time, A.L. had left the active field of politics to devote himself totally to research and writing, which was his real vocation.

Years later in 1979, in the fourth book of his autobiography, *A Man of the Thirties*, A.L. admits, "I deeply regret every moment I spent as a Labour candidate, when a young man, propaganding to make things better." However, he concedes that the political background, and the contact with distinguished leaders throughout Britain, was useful to the historian who followed their careers and subsequent historic events.

A. L. in the 1930's in his first car, campaigning for the Labour Party, with Win Berry seated in front

Chapter Five

POLMEAR MINE

During the summer of 1940, as soon as he had recovered sufficiently from his last operation, A.L. bought a house with an acre of ground on the road to Porthpean with a magnificent view over Charlestown and St. Austell Bay. Known as 101 Porthpean Road, it had previously belonged to the Kelly family, well-known and long established business people in Tregonissey, owning butchers, grocers and Post Office premises there. Mrs. Peters, a married daughter of the Kelly family, lived at the end of Trelawney Road in Tregonissey and was a friend of Mrs. Rowse. It was probably through Mrs. Peters that A.L. knew the Porthpean Road house was for sale. He moved his mother from Robartes Place and the Council house, which she had inhabited for eighteen years, and settled her with a housekeeper at Polmear Mine. He arranged in the house fine pieces of furniture bought in Oxford, and from country house sales, which he attended that summer. 101 Porthpean Road, which he named Polmear Mine, was A.L.'s home in Cornwall from 1940 - 1953. It was the first house that he owned and in which he now felt he could offer hospitality to his college friends. It was the last house on the left hand side going towards Duporth cross-roads and was directly opposite the large white Art Deco styled residence of Charlie Nicholls, proprietor of the St. Austell garage, Truro Road, for whom it had been built. It was named Soulsbyville, after a mining area in America linked to the family. One day, a local friend, Charles Lloyd of Boscundle, observing the house opposite greatly amused A.L. with the pithy remark, "You should call *your* new house All Soulsbyville!" The two men were highly amused by this witty aside, "Charles sinking in the hedge with laughter," said A.L. A poem "Invocation for a Cornish house - Summer 1941" describes the glorious views from the front, the sentinel pine at the gate and the entrance drive which was the old road to the mine closed in the 1870s.

Polmear Mine 101 Porthpean Road. A. L.'s home 1940 - 1953

Polmear Mine, a delightfully designed small house, with its fine entrance hall, dining and drawing rooms, was a haven of quiet after the noisy surroundings of 24 Robartes Place. Rooms were tastefully furnished with the best pieces brought down from Oxford, walls lined with books and modern oil paintings by William Coldstream and Christopher Wood adorned the front hall. From the garden, the lower end of Charlestown Church was visible and white sails of yachts out in the bay.

A.L. moved many books to the house and settled himself upstairs where he furnished a study similar to his own at All Souls. A sale at which he was able to buy more furniture was

Interior Polmear Mine

43

the Rashleigh family one held at Menabilly. He later related that he bought books, furniture and antiques "for a song." One fine piece was a wardrobe made on the estate from wooden chests with late Renaissance poker-work decoration on the front and sides. In a poem about Polmear Mine he reveals that the chair used at his writing desk had been in the front bedroom at Menabilly.

The house, set on level ground, was surrounded by fields and its own gardens. It faced the sea to the south and all along the front of the house was a gravelled terrace on which A.L. placed a pair of Chinese blue and white garden seats either side of the front door. The terrace led on to an enclosed garden area where walls of local stone encompassed shrubs and flower beds linked by flagstones with a sundial in the centre and a wooden bench seat in one corner.

A. L. in the front garden Polmear Mine

Space on the side of the house was reserved for fruit trees, lawn and vegetables with a shrub hedge on the boundary. The garden was secluded and peaceful, ideal for the summer tea-parties Mrs. Rowse so enjoyed with her friends.

Tea Party at Polmear Mine. Mrs Rowse centre

The grounds and garden kept A.L. busy throughout his vacations and when his neighbour, Jack Blake, offered to help keep the garden in order during Oxford terms, A.L. readily accepted. So Jack was employed to help at Polmear Mine and was later persuaded to continue his work at Trenarren, with the unruly garden there.

As well as the view over the surrounding fields to Charlestown, Duporth and the coast, a fine menhyr could be seen from the windows at Polmear Mine. The Longstone was surrounded by fields, formerly Gwallon Downs. It was a tall granite standing stone once surrounded by ancient barrows or burial mounds. A.L. was fascinated by the historical significance of the Longstone and made it the subject of one of his *West Country Stories* published in 1944. The harbour at Charlestown could be reached along a path leading down across the fields from the house. A.L. often walked it, returning home around Brick Hill and past the Lodge at Duporth. From the windows upstairs, he could see the remains of the engine house of Appletree Mine in which his grandfather Rowse had worked.

It was here at Polmear Mine during the war years that A.L. wrote much more poetry. In it he describes the light from the West enriching the line of trees, the Gribben headland lit by a dark red glow and the sky with bands of colour, purples, blues and rose-lit clouds. From "Night Scene in Wartime":

"Sitting at midnight desk I observe the scene,
Moonlight rests
....
On silver dish and inkstand
....
The china horse crops the notional grass."

The Young Writer 1940

45

The early years of the Second World War saw changes in the countryside. King's School, Canterbury was evacuated to the Carlyon Bay Hotel, and the Bayfordbury Hotel opposite, in May 1940. The headmaster, Canon Shirley, took up residence at Trenarren House and became acquainted with his scholarly neighbour. From this time A.L. became familiar with the interior of Trenarren House and its gardens. The two remained friends for many years. In 1964 A.L. dedicated *Christopher Marlowe*, a biography, to John Shirley, Canon of Canterbury, Headmaster of The King's School, 1935-1962 "Friend from Trenarren days." During the war, feeling more secure, A.L. stayed at Polmear Mine and extended friendship to the scholars of King's with lectures on Cornish history, encouraging excursions of discovery into the countryside, with the incentive of a prize for the best essay. Some while later, he arranged a visit to the school by his famous friend Sir Arthur Quiller-Couch.

From the upstairs windows of his new house, with the extensive views out over the sea, A.L. could see the signs of air raids on Plymouth, the searchlights, flares, gun flashes and shell fire, whilst the glow of the fires spread all over the night sky. Nearer to his home, the guns at sea would have threatened the peaceful surroundings. Duporth House and estate were requisitioned as a wartime camp, housing many Indian soldiers who had enlisted in Britain's cause. The war years were mainly spent at Polmear Mine, interspersed with visits to Oxford. During this era, A.L. began and completed his autobiography, *A Cornish Childhood,* his "researches into memory's observant eye." Published in 1942, it was hailed as a masterpiece, selling more than half a million copies over the years and never being out of print in the author's lifetime.

At Polmear Mine, Mrs. Rowse and her housekeeper Janie Harris made their home and kept house when Leslie was away in Oxford. Mrs. Rowse suffered from rheumatism and likely moved to the new house with reluctance missing the neighbourliness of Robartes Place. She is quoted to have said during the early days there, "This ed'n like my 'ouse at all." A.L. always conceded that his mother's dialect was apt and very vivid. During some air raids nearby Mrs. Rowse, downright uncompromising, commented, "Affec' me legs, this 'ere fighters do."

The Cornish have a dry, innate way of understatement. Talking about Hitler and the war with his mother, she replied to A.L. one day, "I dunnaw w'eat I'd do. I b'lieve to tell 'ee the truth, I should be just 'bout 'fraid of 'n."

Mrs Rowse at Polmear Mine

Furthermore her comments on the German bombings, "Dear life. They'll scat it all op before they'm finished." The use of gas masks became a real issue as the war continued. Mrs. Rowse's comment on their appearance was, "W'en Miss 'arris seed me with me nawse bag tied op, she laffed and laffed till she sinked away."

The contents of the house received more sharp-eyed comments too. One of the first was, "We ab'n got nothin' to 'ang nothin' on." The kitchen stove also presented some difficulties, "There's no life nor mirth in 'un," while in her bedroom she complained bitterly about the bed-head. ""I dun't like th' ead of the bed, 'e's too quatty. W'at d'ee quat 'n down like that for?" Her explanation for not appreciating the sheepskin rug laid in her bedroom was, "Me toes d' itch in 'un."

Around the house, A.L. had surrounded himself with lovely things, ceramics, paintings, silver, prints and photographs of the Oxford Commission Survey. Mrs. Rowse commented, " 'ole faaces, good Lor', Gentlemen I s'pawse." One of the paintings was by William Coldstream, an artist whom A.L. commissioned when he met him in Oxford. This painting had been brought to Polmear Mine. It portrayed still life, freesias and a skull symbolising the oncoming war. Leslie asked his mother if she liked the painting. "No, th'ole flowers is fallin' out over the jam jar, like'n ole cat been there scramblin an' pulled 'em out all over." "Then there's 'n ole man's skoll, no I dunt like that one. 'Tis'n awful ole picture." On the mantlepiece was a ceramic figure of a Chinese dragon. Mrs. Rowse did not like this piece either, " 'e's got a mouth like Pascoe got, look at'n, no teeth." Her somewhat scathing comments were likewise directed at the coal fire burning in the grate, "Give that 'ole nub a smack in the faace an' eyes and see if 'e'll blaaze op."

Guests from Oxford could now be invited to stay in Cornwall. Mrs. Rowse's comments about her son's intellectual guests were succinct as usual. "They ben't no cripple in their jaws, nobody w'at d'come 'ere." The illustrations in a Toulouse Lautrec art book caused further exclamation. "What be'm? Actressess. 'Aw my dear life, w'at be'm? Actresses, I s'pawse." A.L. brought his piano back from Oxford for the drawing room at Polmear Mine. He was largely self taught but had considerable skill playing classical music of which he was a fine judge. After one interlude at the piano, A.L. asked his mother if she enjoyed the music. "No, I dunno that I do, " replied Mrs. Rowse. "I'd as soon 'ear an ole dunkey gallopin', as 'ear that."

After barely one year there, as the housekeeper and Mrs. Rowse's companion, Janie Harris died aged fifty years. On the back of a mourning card, A.L. wrote many years later, "Alas, alas, my housekeeper at Polmear, a good woman." His sister, Hilda, home from British Columbia to visit her mother, substituted as housekeeper for a few months but naturally had to return to her own home and family. There followed a series of replacements never staying for long perhaps due to the exacting difficulties of an increasingly infirm old lady and her scholarly son. The situation settled down when Beryl Cloke was employed, and she remained there until Mrs. Rowse died in 1953, then continuing her role as housekeeper when A.L. moved to Trenarren House.

Beryl in the front garden with open view towards Charlestown and the coast.

Laundry Book 1943

It was at Polmear Mine that a succession of stray cats became adopted into the household. Janey was a grey-blue Persian that Beryl had brought from Pentewan as a small kitten. This beautiful cat had a special place in everybody's life at Polmear but while only half-grown it unfortunately ate some poison and died. The next cat was Peter sent, from Bareppa near Mawnan Smith, from one of

Janey - Grey-blue Persian cat at Polmear Mine

A.L.'s friends. Peter was half wild when he first came and spent most of his days exploring the old mine dump nearby. Mrs. Rowse helped to tame him. She was chair-bound by this time with her arthritis and Peter would submit to nursing in her arms.

A Cornish Childhood, published in 1942 was dedicated, "to my mother and the memory of my father." In the preface A.L. reports that his deepest debt is to his mother whose wonderful memory had helped him immensely. He was also thankful for the notebooks in which he had written incidents related by his father about life in Tregonissey village. Richard Rowse could relate from his own father's memories, cottages in Market Hill, St. Austell, stalls set up against the church wall at fair time, cottages opposite the White Hart and fields and gardens where Tregarne Terrace was later built. A.L. claimed that the book was easy to write as, during a period in a London hospital, he had let memories, of his family and home in Cornwall, flood his mind. It evolved easily into a documented account, with the historian's fine edge for accuracy and detail. Written in the upstairs study of Polmear Mine, A.L. was happy in his own first home in the county he adored. Certain passages in the book reveal an intensely sensitive child and adolescent, aware of nature's beauty, church stained glass and architecture and a great love of books and learning.

There were critics of *A Cornish Childhood* from the literary world and the locality but the honesty, detail and beautifully written English prose won great acclaim. A.L. was invited to be a Guest of Honour of the St. Austell Old Cornwall Society, on a special social occasion. Cornish people abroad

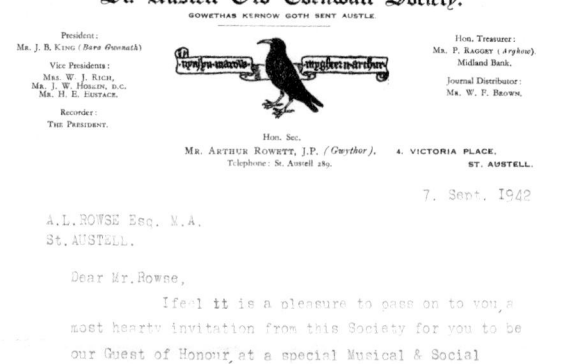

7. Sept. 1942

A.L. Rowse Esq. M.A.
St. Austell.

Dear Mr. Rowse,

I feel it is a pleasure to pass on to you a
most hearty invitation from this Society for you to be
our Guest of Honour at a special Musical & Social
evening to be held on the afternoon of Saturday Jan. 16th/43.
If this date is not suitable for you we will
gladly arrange for the 9th.
Thank you in anticipation. With all good wishes
to mother and yourself.

Yours sincerely,

Arthur Rowett

recalled with nostalgia parts of their own former life in Cornwall, which A.L. had so poignantly brought back, rolling green hills, silver beaches, rugged tors, wind-swept Carn Grey, or the balmier-breezed beach at Porthpean. One emigrant wrote, "Each of these has a niche in the heart of a Cornishman who saw fit to desert his native land." Another complimentary letter stated, "I read your book twice from cover to cover." Other letters from abroad reached Polmear Mine daily as relatives sent copies of *A Cornish Childhood* to family exiles. One from British Columbia related a stay at Crinnis for four or five gloriously happy years. The writer commented, "I got so homesick reading *A Cornish Childhood* that I had to put it aside for several days." A similar letter from a serviceman in Gibraltar said that the writer had read steadily for several hours, pleasure mixed with pain as homesickness overtook him.

Complimentary letters continued to arrive throughout the following years. In 1975, from a letter in the mail at Trenarren, an ardent fan related, "I am enjoying your *Cornish Childhood*. I often 'see' myself as I read, a sensitive, nervous child, very much the odd one out, with a longing for knowledge especially history and language, which no one seemed to understand." In 1994 another letter was received from a Cornishwoman who had read and re-read the book savouring every page. For her it had revived memories of an older generation with a lovely use of Cornish words and expressions. After a walk on the Black Head with a companion, the two ladies had stopped outside Trenarren House. "We looked with respect at the great gates of your home. You are definitely her favourite author and mine too along with the great Charles Dickens."

A.L. owned Polmear Mine for thirteen years and explored the coast and countryside in all directions. Nearby was the farm called Castle Gotha, with the Iron Age ramparts of the first century AD still visible as hedges and ditches in the fields. Evidence had been found of lead and silver smelting on the site. Castle Gotha means "old encampment" in the Cornish language, and from its ramparts a gully ran down to the coast to overlook Silvermine beach on the western edge of St. Austell Bay between Porthpean and Ropehaven. The sides of this gully had been built up with rubble of mine-workings and in the corner of the encampment nearest to Silvermine the remains of a Roman furnace had been traced. Later evidence of this industry came to light when an Anglo-Saxon silver coin, dated 650 AD and minted at Castle Gotha, was offered for auction in a Spink's catalogue.

Interspersed with these local explorations was an unexpected invitation to visit Penrice House for the first time, the seat of the Sawle family, ancient landowners and benefactors of St. Austell. Lady Vyvyan of Trelowarren, on her way to Penrice, recognised A.L. walking past the white entrance gates and took him with her to tea. He recalled that he felt over-awed, had always wanted to see the house so much a part of local history, but he had been too proud to make an approach. Describing the grand house, rooms of lovely furniture, French clocks and old paintings, and meeting Mrs. Sawle, a lady with the natural poise of good breeding, managing stoically in a house beleaguered by war time restrictions, proved a memorable afternoon. From then on, Rosemary Cobbold-Sawle and A.L. became firm friends.

Many friends were invited to Polmear Mine. On A.L.'s ninetieth birthday, Charles Causley sent his congratulations, recalling their first meeting in 1946 at Polmear when A.L. had signed Charles' 1943 copy of *A Cornish Childhood* and had encouraged him towards his own first publication.

By 1953, a larger house was needed to accommodate the vast accumulation of books. Trenarren House was vacant so A.L. sold Polmear Mine and prepared to move to the house of his dreams.

Chapter Six

TRENARREN

There can never be any doubt that Trenarren, the valley, village and House always held a special place in A.L.'s heart. He admitted that he had a "fixation" about the place, the "magic" valley at Trenarren. Going back to his boyhood, he recalled walks to the Blackhead, Hallane beach and picnics on the Ledrah. He also remembered that whilst on a day's outing with his parents and walking down Trenarren lane, Richard Rowse had said, "I daresay Leslie will come to live here one day, but I shan't live to see it," as they viewed Trenarren House over the hedge.

During 1937, while staying at Wardour Castle researching the Arundell archives, A.L., impressed by the magnificence of the house and park, determined to save his money for Trenarren where he could be surrounded by his own trees, flowers and commanding views. In June 1940, while recuperating at Polmear Mine, A.L. records his first bathe at Hallane since his illness, and on his way home visiting the stable block at Trenarren House where an auction was taking place in the courtyard.

It was the success of *A Cornish Childhood,* which virtually opened the door of Trenarren for him. Whilst *Tudor Cornwall,* published in 1941, was widely acclaimed by the academic world, *A Cornish Childhood* had an instant appeal to a massive reading population. Beautifully written in perfect English, it encapsulated the times. By 1944, when this last book had sold over ten thousand copies, A.L. realised that he would be able to afford to live at Trenarren House. In 1952, A.L. decided to look for a new residence. He claimed, "Books drove me out of the charming house at Polmear Mine." By this time he had amassed ten to twelve thousand volumes. It was fortunate that the Hext family, to whom the house belonged, were looking for a new tenant to lease Trenarren House. A.L. moved there during the summer of 1953, with Beryl Cundy his housekeeper. Jack Blake, his gardener agreed to help with the furniture removers. The south-facing house overlooked the sloping lawns and gardens with immense rhododendron trees at the bottom and the sea beyond, an exquisite setting. It was the "magic" valley.

The house was described, by the agent, as a "Late Georgian Country and Seaside Residence." It had nearly thirty rooms, including servants quarters and two large attics on the second floor, so the problem of storing books was solved. Rooms at the back of the house surrounded a covered yard and included the staff bedrooms, one of which had been adapted and used as a chapel by Canon Shirley, headmaster of King's School, Canterbury who had resided at Trenarren during the evacuation of his school to Cornwall. The chapel room entrance could be reached by a set of steps, set into the back drive, possibly a former servants' entrance. A bell, mounted high up on the south west side of the house overlooking the back courtyard, had been used to call villagers to services in the chapel.

Trenarren House was a large residence for two people. The lease included a stable block, comprising a garage, stalls for horses, a saddle room and harness room with its own fireplace and chimney, as well as a gardener's cottage in the village, called Myrtle Cottage. The garden and grounds extended to almost nine acres including a hard tennis court and a lower kitchen garden with orchard. The house, sheltered by fine trees and plantations, was an ideal retreat for a man whose happiest time was when he was alone to think, read and write.

The Hext family had owned land in Trenarren, which included fish cellars at Ropehaven and tenements as far as the Blackhead, from the seventeenth century. The first manor house was built around the end of that century when the Hext property had been augmented by more land. It was situated on a lower level to the present house, again facing south. In 1721 there is a mention of Thomas Hext of Trenarren and Lord of the manor of Tewington, one of St. Austell's three Domesday manors. During the eighteenth century, there were further tenements, orchards, gardens and fish cellars at Hallane added to the Hext estate. John Hext, married in 1799, set about building a new house and a further transaction of a land sale in 1801 between Thomas Carlyon of Tregrehan and Thomas Hext was probably the deciding factor to build on the site higher up the valley.

Gothic stone arch from the old house.

The old house was taken down and a date stone of 1805 was set in the wall of the cellars of the new Trenarren House. Some stonework from the old house was brought up the hill and used on the new Hext property. The Gothic stone entrance arch to the old manor was incorporated into the back of the house, with its heavy oak door leading out to the covered yard. Two round and scrolled granite embellishments, probably from the gables of the old roof, were set on columns forming the entrance to the stable block.

The new Trenarren House was built of mellow Pentewan stone with six well-proportioned windows in its Georgian frontage. From the middle downstairs window, one could step out on to the front terrace with its stunning views. At the back were the kitchens and servants quarters with a back drive linking to the coach house. On the east side of the house, facing the road, was the entrance with a small porch. Creeper and shrubs were planted here, eventually covering the whole of that side.

Two views of Trenarren House about 1900

The first owner John Hext does not appear to have lived in his new house very much. A series of leases letting the property ensued when subsequently the Hext family moved their main residence to Restormel Park, Lostwithiel, a Gothic Georgian house under the shadow of Restormel Castle. Here the Hexts pursued a fine life style of country living. They played an integral role in the town of Lostwithiel, a stannary town of some importance compared with St. Austell , which was just a small township around the parish church. Trenarren valley and properties were shared between the Hext and Sawle families. During the 1850's one of the branches of the Hext family came back to Trenarren House. This was Thomas Hext, who with a large family of five daughters and six sons, was succeeded by his son Arthur in 1881. Arthur had three daughters, so a nephew became the heir and he was the last of the family to live there.

Into the twentieth century a number of families took leases on Trenarren, mostly for fourteen years at the average rent of £150 per annum. In 1943 the Blackhead Rifle Range used by the Cornish Territorial Army Association had a seven year lease for £12 per annum but by the following year the Shirley family were in residence. Two further short leases followed until 1953 when A.L. became the tenant, remaining so for the next forty-four years.

There is no doubt that this tenant loved his new home, for its solitude and peace but it was the gardens, spinney and orchard which greatly captivated his heart. In the early days that summer there was much to clear, for in Cornwall, Nature soon takes over. The lawns at the front had developed into a hayfield, thickly matted with weeds and corrugated with mole hills. A.L. had contacted the Urban District Council to organise a machine to cut the grass but on arrival it, "Chugged, snorted and spluttered" and refused to tackle the long grass. Not the most patient of men, A.L. was furious at the delay but had to wait for it to be hand-scythed before it could be mown. Hedges and paths had to be reinstated piecemeal. It was a huge task and A.L. relied greatly on Jack Blake in those early years, especially as he had to return to Oxford during term time. No major alterations were made in the gardens but an immense programme of weed clearance beneath trees and shrubs was necessary.

At the bottom of the lawn, behind the massive rhododendron bushes and a retaining wall was the well-house for the water supply to the house. The deep well was fed by a never-failing spring of water, which appeared again at the pump down in the village and supplied all Trenarrren inhabitants, ultimately pouring over the cliff below the Vans on to the beach below. To get water to Trenarren House, an engine was used to pump it up to storage tanks by the old stables but it caused so much frustration and trouble that the water supply was switched to the upper well near the coach house where the water flow was considerably better. This system continued until the late 1960s when the mains supply was piped down from the cross-roads at Lobb's shop on the way to Pentewan. Below the well-house was the area termed the Paddock, also completely overgrown when A.L. took over, but formerly a garden supplying cut flowers for the house. Across an intersecting lane below the Paddock, water was piped to the greenhouses in the kitchen garden. Here Jack Blake grew tomatoes and vegetables and extended his gardening down some steps overhung by a couple of immense fig trees to the lower kitchen garden, and beyond that to the orchard, which included several old varieties of apple trees.

On the western side of the property, above the upper walk, was a wooded area with large pines bordering the fields of Trevissick farm. A.L. termed this, "The jungle or wilderness." Here it is said he spent many hours often alone and working feverishly to clear his system of some annoyance. Jack Blake related that, when A.L. had a tax demand, he would come out in sombre mood. "Today we'll do so and so, I've had a tax demand Jack and it has upset me," he would say. It was to the "jungle" area that A.L. would retire if he really wanted to get away from people or to think out the sequence of the next book. During the summer evenings this area was often bathed in a honey-coloured glow and had a splendid view south-westerly away to the Vans. At the end nearest to the sea there was the old cinder tennis court and that was another project that A.L. and Jack tackled, clearing the grass which had overgrown it and planting shrubs.

The original kitchen gardens of the house, still a part of the property in 1953, was a wedge-shaped area in one of the fields alongside the coach house. It remained from the days when a large family and a household of servants needed plenty of garden produce. It was a derelict garden when A.L. took over the property. Everything had gone to seed, grass, docks and brambles. From it, through the two granite posts with heads coiled like snail-whorls, a track led to the coach house or along the overgrown drive to the back entrance.

When Trenarren House was being built in 1805, it had been the intention to make the main entrance at the fork in the road by Trevissick junction, where an entrance with splendidly curved herring-bone stone walls on either side was planned.. The two fields beyond were to be transformed into parkland, as on other country estates, an appropriate and grand approach to the house. This plan, however, never materialised.

Throughout his tenure at Trenarren House, the garden was a delightful place for A.L., though innate impatience over-ruled on more than one occasion when growth invaded, and he had to spend two or three weeks with Jack, hacking back the jungle. He was easily riled at the recalcitrant garden tools, rakes, steps, long-handled shears, which seemed to have a life of their own ready to thwart his progress. There would be some bad language, not always mild, as A.L. attacked nettles and brambles, or searched for the missing implements. Once, with both hands heaped with bulbs and trowel, a rake under arm and a roll of garden twine he made his way in characteristically haphazard fashion around the bushes to cross the garden. When he reached the far side, and glanced behind, he saw that the whole packet of cord had become entwined around camellia and azalea bushes on his blundered course. He was not amused.

Writing to Jack from Pasadena, California in 1966 he said, "I don't want to leave Cornwall next year till the end of September. I've for long wanted to spend the whole of September at home, gardening." Another year later he wrote to Jack, "I am never so well as in the summer working in the open air at Trenarren." In his poem *Summer Work* A.L. described himself in his garden:

"Striped to the waist, cope with weeds
      Thistles, docks, couch-grass, uncut hedges."

Another poem, *November Sunrise* includes:

      "Between me and the sea
      A screen of filigree
      Dark and skeletal trees
      Erect a formal frieze."

The Beeches at Trenarren, Trenarren Winter and *New Year in Cornwall* were poems inspired by the garden.

> "Now over the magic valley
> Through the trees' leafless screen
> Rises the silver moon
> Ravished but serene."

The librarian of the Huntington who had been a guest of A.L.'s at Trenarren had taken coloured slides of the garden. He had showed them back in California at a later date to his host, who wrote to Jack, "Everybody wonders why I ever leave such a beautiful place, but I need to make money to keep Trenarren. I shouldn't be able to do it if it weren't for America."

At the front of the house was a wide, level and gravelled terrace, a truly idyllic sitting area. Paths led from there around the garden in a circular route. Across the road from the main entrance was the spinney, a triangular and naturally wooded area of mixed trees covered with primroses and bluebells in the Spring and tailing off to the Ledra.

A.L. wrote many poems about Trenarren and that he felt passionately about his home there is no doubt.

> "Bring my books about me
> Take them down from the wall
> Stack them all around me
> Buttressed against a fall."

From these poems describing the mottled silver, grey-green stonework, the violet hues sometimes evident in the glass of the old window panes we appreciate A.L.'s passion for the place. He once wrote, "It is the quality of the light, the various lighting here that moves me most. The glory of the first faint rose flush of dawn, pale gleams of sunrise in the east, tracing through the trees in the Spinney, and the honey-gold and lemon shafts of the evening sunset, silhouetted by the trees on the upper paths touch inexpressible springs." The extreme beauty of his garden was ever apparent and a continual delight to a man who knew every tree, shrub and corner of the place just as he knew his books within the house.

When A.L. moved into Trenarren in 1953, it was a major operation and occupied several days. Jack Blake recalled how he was enlisted to deposit large numbers of books, ten or twelve thousand, but with A.L. over-seeing the whereabouts. The back stairs were built up vertically from the top downwards until each step could take no more, the books relying on support from the ones above. "The stairs were practically impassable," said Jack. The two attics stored cardboard boxes of memorabilia brought down from Oxford, press cuttings, manuscripts, church guides, history magazines, suitcases, tea chests and unrequired household articles.

The Library - Trenarren. Photo by Charles Woolf - Newquay

The Library at Trenarren was part of an extension to the original house and built about 1840. Known originally as the Drawing Room, it had a fine decorative cornice around the ceiling and a wide southward window overlooking the garden. A.L. directed the arrangement of furniture and rugs brought from Oxford as well as from Polmear Mine, laying a large pale peach and gold Susuch, a pale green Aubusson and a French needlework carpet in the Library. On these were placed the Louis Sixteenth tapestry sofa and Louis Philippe tapestry chairs bought to celebrate the move into the grand old house. Two high arched wall embrasures were shelved for books from floor to ceiling and the stone built fireplace was replaced by a marble Regency one.

Paintings and portraits could now be shown to best advantage. One of these, a painting by Christopher Wood entitled Green Hills and completed in 1926 was the first that A.L. had ever bought. He had purchased it from Ryman's in the High, Oxford with earnings from tutorials. It showed the Cornwall that he knew, the intensity of colour in the landscape, moors, fields, a church tower and a white triangle of a sand burrow. A.L. once told Jack at Polmear Mine, "If there is ever a fire Jack, take my Christopher Wood and get outside." The gallery had priced the painting at 30 guineas but had conceded to sell it for £27.10 (£27.50). It was one of the best investments that A.L. ever made.

The dining room, with the window that could be opened onto the terrace, was carpeted with Persian rugs. The dining chairs had been bought in Oxford but the table purchased locally from the owner for £1 when A.L. was living at Polmear. It had been discovered, stored in a garden shed. Paintings in this room, the only room in the house where there were no books, included an early water colour sketch of the medieval chapel at Hall Farm, Bodinnick by John Piper, who had been introduced to A.L. by John Betjeman. On the far wall a Gainsborough painting of Sir Francis Bassett of Tehidy adjoined the chimney-breast.

The Dining Room - Trenarren. Photo by Charles Woolf - Newquay

The housekeeper's room on the side of the house was mostly furnished with his mother's belongings from the house in Tregonissey. A pine dresser, or "buffet" as the Cornish called it, displayed old jugs, plates and teapots. There was also the christening cup and saucer painted on the side in gold letters, Alfred Leslie Rowse, December 3rd 1903, no doubt a present from Uncle and Auntie Rowe's china shop. A pine table, chairs and a Victorian wall clock had all belonged to his parents. Another possession of his father's, which A.L. brought to Trenarren, was Richard Rowse's pine sea-chest which he had used when he went to South Africa and which had formerly belonged to his own father.

A fine Roger Wearn inlaid mahogany longcase clock made at St. Erth was placed in the hall with a Dutch engraving of Sir Francis Drake bought from the sale at Menabilly in 1940 hung on the wall opposite. Various prints of Cornwall and many of Oxford were hung around the house, and the Ibach piano brought from Polmear Mine installed in the hall. Jack Blake recalled A.L.'s impatience with the length of time it took to get Trenarren as he wanted. Apparently the grandfather clock struck at odd hours for several days and the French Louis XVI clock in the dining room also played up. A.L. complained that even the picture hooks had a life and mind of their own.

The Hall - Trenarren.

Upstairs, A.L. furnished the middle room at the front of the house facing the sea, as his bedroom. With a Chinese silk wall-hanging behind his bed, he faced a fireplace at the other end of the room which he claimed had been made out of the oak panelling from the dining room of the former house, and painted. As well as other bedroom furniture, two Victorian rosewood armchairs were set on either side of the fireplace and alongside his bed stood a bookcase which contained his favourite books and poetry volumes. The guest bedroom in the newer wing contained the wardrobe bought at the Menabilly sale in 1940. A lady's dressing table and marquetry chair, also from this sale, stood in front of the window. Adjoining this room was a small bedroom, probably an earlier dressing room, which became known as his brother George's room. On the mantelpiece here was placed the Staffordshire china figure of Red Riding Hood, a reminder of Tregonissey days where it belonged on the mantelpiece in the sitting room.

The Guest Bedroom - Trenarren.   Photo by Charles Woolf - Newquay

Most of the other bedrooms, with the exception of one for Beryl, were used as studies. Into each one were allocated the books, categorised into sections, for various bookcases. All the corridors housed shelves, bookcases and boxes. A.L. always retained a wonderful memory regarding the location of his books and could pinpoint which room, which bookcase and relevant shelf position. Occasionally he would telephone from Oxford asking Beryl to locate a certain book that he needed. It was invariably where he had said.

The studies and other main rooms in Trenarren were tastefully furnished with paintings, ceramics and objets d'art. Other artists' work included Lowry, Felix Kelly, John Aldridge, Ceria Cedric Morris, William Coldstream, W. Barns-Graham, Lionel Miskin and an early John Martin. Two seventeenth century Italian apothecary jars, one dated 1621, Staffordshire figures, Coalport vases of cherubs pushing grape-hung barrows still retaining their price ticket of 7/6 (37p) when purchased, adorned the mantelpieces, ledges and window sills.

At work in upstairs study - 1967 Photo by Charles Woolf - Newquay

This was Trenarren in its early days, with A.L. and Beryl as its residents until the former went to Oxford or later America. Then the house was closed up and Beryl lived in Myrtle Cottage in the village. Jack Blake worked there when his shifts at the telephone exchange in St. Austell permitted, combining gardening with indoor tasks. In the early days coal was delivered and deposited in the coal cellar via a chute in the back yard. It was one of Jack's tasks to light the boiler there in winter.

From Polmear Mine came a third important inhabitant of Trenarren House. It was Peter, the white cat brought as a gift to A.L. while he was living at Polmear, who settled happily enough there but spent most of the days hunting and exploring the mining dumps nearby. The transition to Trenarren is described in *Peter, The White Cat of Trenarren,* which A.L. wrote in 1974. The new place was a paradise for cats and the author vividly describes daily routine in the early days interspersing garden incidents with household ones, Oxford terms and periods in America as they affected Peter. The cat accompanied A.L. into the garden, settled on his lap, sometimes on his manuscripts and accompanied him to the bedroom, often sleeping beside him throughout the night. Some beautifully descriptive passages of Trenarren are included in Peter's biography.

A. L. with Peter on the front garden terrace

A. L. with Peter on kitchen window sill - Trenarren

From 1953 onwards, numerous guests were invited to Trenarren House where A.L. acted as host and guide to the Cornish countryside. Early friends included Geoffrey Grigson, Cornish author from Pelynt, and a Leicestershire historian friend Jack Simmons. Numerous contemporaries from All Souls, the Warden, Manciple and Fellows were also guests and as America came to play a more important part in his lecture schedule and research programme other contacts and friends from across the Atlantic enjoyed A.L.'s hospitality at Trenarren.

Chapter Seven

CORNWALL AND FRIENDS

Amongst the village children at Tregonissey it was generally acknowledged that Leslie Rowse was "different". He joined in some of the early games outside in the road by the shop but with his preference for books and reading becoming more and more apparent, childhood pastimes were soon dropped in favour of literature, the path of learning and the inner life of the mind.

Christened at the Parish Church, St. Austell and accompanying his mother to services there, A.L. realised an early appreciation of music. He loved the singing and organ music. In *A Cornish Childhood* he related that he spent some of his free time as a child sitting up a tree pushing and pulling branches as though they were pedals and stops on the church organ, meanwhile singing loudly in accompaniment. He was later confirmed by Bishop Burrows of Truro into the Anglican Church and became a member of the church choir, under the leadership and training of the organist. His beautiful treble voice was trained and developed and with his gift of singing A.L. progressed to head chorister, taking part in recitals on Sunday evenings and solo performances both in St. Austell and around the district.

John and Reg Clark

Coinciding with A.L.'s early years at the County School, were two brothers John and Reg Clark who had come to live in St. Austell, their father having been made an Income-Tax inspector in the town. Having both been choirboys in London, they became members of the choir at Holy Trinity church and also pupils at the County School alongside A.L. These became his first real friends, John the elder, "A quiet sensitive lad became a loyal friend. We were inseparable," wrote A.L. in 1942. "Neither of us interested in games and enjoying our own jokes and company." Choir outings and picnics were shared with John and Reg and exchange visits were made to each other's home. A.L. was very anxious about their visit to Tregonissey. He had never before been allowed to invite anyone there to tea, and he was very aware of the combined two old cottages of his home, with no amenities, compared to the bow-fronted house at Highfield Avenue, in which the two brothers lived.

At the County School, John and A.L. continued their friendship until after the Senior Oxford examinations when at seventeen years of age, instead of continuing further with his education, John was sent back to work in London, much to A.L.'s dismay at losing the only real friend he had had. Writing back to his friend in Cornwall describing his work, near the Royal Exchange, John wrote, "There are some most exquisite pictures which I am sure you would love to see." He also referred to his brother Reg, who had lately been made a prefect at the County School, and to Miss Medland whom he claimed his friend, "Used to play up." Good wishes for A.L.'s Oxford examinations were

John Clark
A. L.'s first school friend at
St. Austell County School

included. The camaraderie which they shared was evident and John's untimely death from pneumonia shortly afterwards was a devastating blow to A.L. In his autobiography, he wrote with compassion and tenderness of the unfinished letter from his friend found amongst John's belongings, and forwarded later by John's parents.

A photograph of John taken in front of the school was kept as a cherished memory. In 1942 A.L. wrote, "Through all the years and their subsequent experiences of friendship and death, of long illness, unhappiness and loneliness I have always kept that little photograph between the pages of my Prayer Book at the service for the Burial of the Dead." This prize, won by A.L. at fourteen years of age, was Bishop Phillpott's award for examination in the prayer book for achieving first place in the senior division, December 1917. The photograph remained in that page throughout A.L.'s life. He wrote on the back, "Dear John Clark, my first school friend, St. ACS, died in London at 17." Dates were added in A.L.'s handwriting from 1980 to 1994 most likely after he had re-read the particular passage marked by John's photograph.

Early St. Austell Friends

Exploring the locality on foot around St. Austell as a young man, A.L. found that Luxulyan was a place which drew him back there time and time again. Early poems echo his love of the area, the church in the village and the wonderful valley below it. Once in his room at All Souls, he experienced a sudden nostalgia for Luxulyan, "The tang of the moorland air, scents, bracken, gorse, heather, exotic ferns every variety that prick their ears up in all the crevices and crannies of the valley."

It was to Luxulyan that A.L. had walked with his earliest and best friends, Len Tippett, Noreen Sweet and later Charles Henderson. The first two were contemporaries at the County School, both academically talented, who enjoyed the Debating and Literary Societies as well as the dramatic productions with A.L. Len and Noreen remained friends with him throughout their lifetime, corresponding regularly and visiting when circumstances permitted both in Oxford and Cornwall. They knew the Rowse family members at Tregonissey and kept in touch with Mrs. Rowse throughout her life. Noreen married Christopher Vivian in 1939. A.L. admired her scholarship and admitted that she had been the only woman that he might have married. She died in 1993.

During the years when politics were foremost in A.L.'s career, friendship developed with the Browning-Lyne family, the head of which was the editor of the *Cornish Guardian* newspaper at Bodmin. In correspondence, A.L. thanks Norman Browning-Lyne for sympathetic reference to his political stance. He later claimed that only a few people like the Lyne family, Noreen Sweet and Claude Berry really knew and understood. Letters and articles to the *Cornish Guardian* conveyed A.L.'s standpoint to local readers. Writing to Norman Browning-Lyne about his political commitments, he mentioned that he had turned down a travelling Fellowship of £1000 for one year. In a comment dated 1982, A.L. pencilled alongside, "Fancy missing that for the sake of politics." In 1938, after his operation at Universtiy College Hospital, A.L. wrote to Norman Lyne referring to dreams of beloved beaches in Cornwall, Trenarren, Perranporth, Pendower and Porth Hellick on the Isles of Scilly, "Where Charles (Henderson) and I had the most delicious bathes in the cool, clear water. The thought of it kept me going."

Sir Arthur Quiller-Couch 1863-1944
"Q"

As a young pupil of the Elementary School at Carclaze, A.L. read and was greatly captivated by the adventures in the story of *The Splendid Spur* by Sir Arthur Quiller-Couch. One could say that it was his first glimpse of Oxford history, and it was certainly this book which encouraged him to read the other works of "Q" as he became known, and which were the foundation of a lifelong admiration of the author.

For many years, A.L. would not have been aware that Quiller-Couch lived across St. Austell Bay on the other side of the Gribben headland, at Fowey. In 1915, however, having won a scholarship to the County School, St. Austell, A.L. met "Q" as one of the governing body. As chairman of the County Education Committee, Quiller-Couch often visited the new school at St. Austell and such was the academic success and achievement of A.L. that he received several prizes, presented by "Q". One of these, *Studies in Literature* encouraged further reading, sights of Oxford, and an admiration that inspired thoughts of following in "Q's" footsteps as a writer.

It was at Easter 1922, having been proposed to enter for the English School at Christ Church, that an interview was arranged for A.L. to seek advice from the great academic. In *A Cornish Childhood*, the author describes his interest and delight at meeting Quiller-Couch for the first time, in his own home at Fowey. The two sat in the book-lined study of "The Haven", overlooking the harbour, Polruan and the open sea. "Q" was dressed in a rather archaic manner, redolent of Charles I, breeches and long stockings

The Haven "Q's" home at Fowey

reported A.L. The discussion was centred round the scholarship and the competition it evoked. "Q" mentioned that he had previously coached a young gentleman of a famous family for a similar scholarship, which he had not won. Maybe "Q" was testing A.L.'s mettle, for the latter recalled, "I remember registering to myself, doggedly, defiantly, 'Well, we'll see'." Before he left "The Haven", A.L. had been advised to attempt the scholarship, which he did that summer, and was successful. News of his achievement was reported nationally in the newspapers and both County School and the local community basked in the glory of this unique achievement.

On the occasion of the Christmas Speech Day at the County School in 1922, the enactment of a play adapted from "Q's" novel *Troy Town* took place. A.L. had written it at the headmaster's request before leaving for his first term at Oxford, to be produced by the Staff. The dialogue had been

Sir Arthur Quiller-Couch

easy to adapt and the dialect of the inhabitants of Troy Town was perfect for the characters, but this was to be expected admitted A.L. because "Q's" dialect was perfect. He was a Cornishman and "belonged". The school performance was a great success. "Q" arrived for in full evening dress, and in taking the curtain call took A.L. on to the stage with him to share the applause for this dramatic version of his book.

There would have been regular correspondence between Quiller-Couch and the young Cornish scholar in his first years at Oxford. "Q" was the

70

emissary for three Cornish friends who wished to remain anonymous but on more than one occasion included three £5 notes as a help towards Oxford expenses, in recognition of the credit being achieved, and its reflection on the County. "Q" retained a great interest in the career of his younger friend, and nothing delighted A.L. more than being able to visit Fowey during the vacations.

'Q" wearing plus fours and gaiters in the street of Fowey

After the publication of *A Cornish Childhood* in 1942, A.L. was again summoned to Fowey to meet "Q". At this time the older man was writing his own autobiography so the two authors shared a common interest. A.L. admitted that he had not the inclinations of "Q" who had spent so much time with public work in Cornwall. By 1942, having finished with active politics, he determined to pursue a writing career at all costs. He had always acknowledged "Q's" great literary skill, and especially admired the Cornish folklore and dialect stories, which he integrated into his works. A.L. also admired "Q" as being old-fashioned and chivalrous. On the margins of the pages of his "Q" books, A.L.'s comments were endearing. "Dear old 'Q'," "What a gent 'Q' was!" and another, "Darling old boy 'Q'," showed the great affection he held for his mentor and friend. A.L. appreciated that "Q" had experience of the best of Cornwall, its folklore and stories, the days before cars, a thorough knowledge of the coast from sailing and technical details of all kinds of ships and sailing, complete nautical expertise.

After Sir Arthur's death in 1944, A.L. continued to visit his widow and daughter Foy at "The Haven". On August 4th 1948, a memorial to Sir Arthur Quiller-Couch was unveiled at Penleath Point, Hall Walk, Bodinnick, across the river from Fowey in a commanding position overlooking the harbour and estuary. A.L., although invited, did not want to attend fearing that grief for his friend would overwhelm him. In a

FOWEY,

4th August, 1948

MEMORIAL TO
SIR ARTHUR QUILLER-COUCH
AT PENLEATH POINT, HALL WALK, BODINNICK

Two monuments, one commemorating the men of the Parishes of Fowey and Lanteglos who gave their lives in the war of 1939-1945, and the other in memory of Sir Arthur Quiller-Couch, will be unveiled on the land presented by Lieut. Colonel Peter Shakerley, R.A., on SATURDAY, SEPTEMBER 4TH., at 3 p.m., when a service of dedication will be conducted by the Lord Bishop of Truro.

It will give everyone great pleasure if you are able to be present on this occasion ; and the Committee direct me to inform you that arrangements will be made for the conveyance of visitors arriving at the Fowey side of Bodinnick Ferry.

N. A. HOCKEN,
Hon. Secretary.

A. L. seated at the "Q" memorial

subsequent meeting with Foy at "The Haven", A.L. recalled that she understood completely. They went into the drawing room to see the memorial on the crest of the hill.

In 1988, A.L. published *Quiller-Couch, A Portrait of Q,* dedicating the book to Daphne du Maurier in common admiration of their old friend. Having been presented with a copy of that book, "Autographed with affection for Valery by her old Friend the Author," and discussing its subject one day, I realised that A.L. had never been to the "Q" memorial. In April of that year he agreed that he would like to see it, so along with Phyllis Cundy, his housekeeper, we crossed by ferry to Bodinnick and having parked as close as possible to the Hall Walk we made our way to the headland.

Along the route we met David Treffry of Place with his niece. They had already reached the monument and were returning but such was A.L.'s delight at seeing his close friend so unexpectedly that there was no option except to retrace steps. The photograph taken that afternoon shows his

72

delight and happiness. He studied the plaque, remarking on its fine workmanship, and discoursed at length of "Q's" great literary ability and influence in English literature. It was compelling listening, and an unforgettable occasion for us all.

From one of A.L's Cornish poems is a tribute:

At Fowey, For 'Q'

Valerian, privet, escallonia
Look seaward from the Haven
He will come no more home to.
There is the green boat laid up for good.

It was through A.L.'s intervention that the characteristic portrait of "Q", by Henry Lamb was arranged, and it now hangs in the County Museum.

Charles Henderson 1900 - 1933

Sir Arthur Quiller- Couch had befriended the young schoolboy, encouraging and directing his literary career, but it was Charles Henderson, whose family lived at Penmount, near Truro who became a close contemporary friend of A.L.

Most probably from his County School days, A.L. would have heard of the name Charles Henderson and his study of Cornish manuscripts, documents and knowledge of ancient sites throughout the county. However, it was not until they met in 1928 at Oxford that acquaintance and real friendship developed through their Cornish roots.

Charles Henderson's early life at Penmount had brought many introductions to the aristocratic families of Cornwall, their libraries and documents, inspiring in him a quest for Cornish history. In *A Cornishman Abroad*, A.L. noted,

"From the time he was a boy, Charles had been passionately interested in documents, transcribing, translating, collecting wherever he went."

Charles' main hobby had been searching out and collecting deeds, leases and documents that shed light on the past. The result was that he had a unique familiarity with mediaeval Cornwall and knew the countryside as no one had ever known, every parish church, the farms, bridges, fields and people. He tramped over the landscape, over hedges and ditches. A.L. claimed, "Nothing daunted him in his pursuit of the Cornish past." It is no wonder he acclaimed that Charles was the first among Cornish scholars. Henry Jenner, president of the Royal Institution of Cornwall, and first Grand Bard of the Cornish Gorsedd, had known Charles Henderson since he was a young boy, then avidly interested in archaeology, collecting data and surveying plans. Hamilton Jenkin had accompanied Charles exploring the Cornish countryside as did William Stephens of Newquay, another renowned local antiquarian. So the young Henderson had had an immense advantage of knowing these early scholars.

Charles Henderson achieved First Class History Honours at New College, Oxford, travelled and lived in Italy for a while before becoming an extra mural lecturer for Cornwall at Exeter University. It was in 1928, having returned to Corpus Christi Oxford as a Fellow that he was introduced to A.L. Rowse, whilst dining at All Souls. After that occasion they met frequently, sharing a great common interest in, and love of, Cornish history. "He was vastly learned about Cornwall," wrote A.L., "what a marvellous education that was as we walked or bussed all around Cornwall during vacations." Charles was socially more at ease than A.L. and was well connected. A.L.

Charles Henderson on the left

remembered staying at Penmount, his first ever country house weekend, with forays into the local parish and exploring Castle An Dinas, the large Iron Age hill-top camp above the Goss Moor. The two Cornish scholars visited Mawnan where the poet John Masefield and his wife were staying, and also Lis Escop to have supper with Bishop Frere. In September 1928, Charles was made a bard of the Cornish Gorsedd, taking the name "Mab Hendra" "Son of the old town" from Henry Jenner the Grand Bard, in recognition as an historical researcher of outstanding gifts.

Life at Oxford in the company of Charles Henderson became more enriched for A.L. The two shared walks in the college grounds and the Oxfordshire countryside, another visit this time to meet John Buchan and his wife who lived at Elsfield Manor, and train journeys between Cornwall and Oxford, greatly enjoyed by both. When A.L. left Oxford to lecture at the London School of Economics, visiting was curtailed but the two still met, though infrequently in Cornwall. Charles, a generous host, invited some of A.L.'s friends to stay at Penmount, sharing his enthusiasm and extraordinary knowledge of the county. A.L. in return arranged a

Mr. Charles Henderson (right) at the first Cornish Gorsedd at Boscawen-Un.
1928

visit and took Charles to see Methrose in Luxulyan, an ancient manor house with an enclosed courtyard which Charles had never had the chance to visit.

In July 1932, the two friends visited the Isles of Scilly, staying at Tregarthen's Hotel on St. Mary's. They explored the antiquities of the islands, those chambered tombs and settlements, which are a predominant feature there, along with the Abbey gardens at Tresco. During his stay, A.L. bought and read another "Q" novel, *Major Vigoureux*, whose subject matter centred around the garrison on St. Mary's.

The following summer, Charles married Isobel Munro, daughter of the rector of Lincoln College and left for a tour of Italy. In September he died there and was buried in Rome in the Testaccio cemetery. On returning from a visit to the north of England, A.L. recorded, "The dire news of

Charles Henderson's death." His tribute to him, printed in the *West Briton,* September 28th 1933, was an epic, combining an account of his prolific writing, studies and manuscript archives with A.L.'s own tribute. "I most admired his combination of strength with gentleness and restraint ~ ~ the most pure and good nature I have ever known, wise tolerance and the gifts of discernment and certainty of conviction."

The late Mr. Charles Henderson, of Penmount, Truro, a Fellow of Corpus Christi College, Oxford.
[Photo: Soame, Oxford.

Six months later another article for the *West Briton* appeared in which A.L. outlined a memorial for Charles Henderson. This was to take the form of a book compiled from all those original deeds and documents and the best of his articles and studies, work he had completed, entitled, *Essays in Cornish History.* A.L. had agreed to edit it along with Isobel, Charles' widow, and with a preface by "Q". The appeal was successful. As well as publishing the book, enough money was collected to furnish a room to house the documents and transcripts of Charles Henderson, bequeathed to the Royal Institution of Truro.

A long poem, Extempore Memorial, was written as a moving tribute to his friend's untimely death.

"Who is this that moves when the leaves move
By Tresillian Bridge, past Pencalenick and St. Clement's Cross?
What dear ghost is this comes revisiting his former places?
I who remember keep watch in vain."

A.L. kept in tough with the Henderson family and corresponded regularly with Charles' sister Christabel all her life.

Dr. William Stephens 1866 - 1945

It was through Charles Henderson that A.L. was introduced to Dr. William Stephens of Hayne, Newquay, another antiquarian and collector of documents and manuscripts of his own area. He was an avid recorder and kept his trained eye on any alterations or discoveries within the countryside. He corresponded with A.L. on matters of local importance. There was some concern locally over the new road being constructed in the Rialton Valley, preservation of the remains of the Celtic cross there and the encroachment of the Priory grounds. Excavators at work on the new aerodrome at Carnanton had revealed slate coffins containing skeletons and Colonel Williams, the owner of the estate, had contacted William Stephens to investigate. Dr. Stephens valued A.L.'s opinion and contacted him with references and queries about academic sources. They visited seventeenth century manor houses and old farms together.

During the late 1920s and early 1930s, William Stephens, Charles Henderson and A.L. Rowse formed a triangle of local historians all of whom shared the delight in the quest of Cornish history.

Claude Berry   1895 -1966

A man of ideals for his native Cornwall, Claude Berry had shared a very similar home background to A.L. Claude's father had been a carpenter earning £1 a week, very similar to the wages of Richard Rowse, the clay labourer. Reminiscing of his early life in Padstow, Claude compared "the brave endeavours of the working class women managing on those low wages" with others in similar villages throughout Cornwall.

Brought up in a small cottage on the quay-side at Padstow, and from the Elementary School there, Claude Berry progressed on a scholarship to the County School at Bodmin, eight years ahead of his counterpart in St. Austell. From the County School, and after a brief interlude as an unqualified teacher, Claude joined the army during the First World War. After service in France with the Duke of Cornwall's Light Infantry, he proceeded to London University to study journalism for two years. Returning to Cornwall in 1921, he joined the staff of the *Cornish Guardian* at Bodmin, later taking an appointment in Fleet Street, where he reported in the Parliamentary Press Gallery of the House of Commons. Thus he acquired an inside knowledge of the world of politics but ill health forced him to return to Cornwall, rejoining the staff at Bodmin. In 1931, Claude joined the *West Briton* at Truro, eventually becoming its editor in 1947,until his retirement.

TELEPHONE NO'S.:—TRURO 600 AND 601. (2 LINES).　　　　　TELEGRAMS: 'BRITON, TRURO.'

"The West Briton & Cornwall Advertiser"

TRURO　　　　　　Newspaper, Limited.

Largest Guaranteed	MEMBER A.B.C.	BEST ADVERTISING MEDIUM.
Circulation of any	ESTABLISHED 1810.	Published in Truro every Monday and Thursday, Monday's Edition 1d.;
Cornish Newspaper.		Thursday's Edition 2d.

ALL COMMUNICATIONS
MUST BE ADDRESSED
TO THE EDITOR OR TO
THE MANAGER :: ::

"West Briton Office,"

TRURO.

Saturday, Jan. 4ᵗʰ, 1941

Between the two World Wars, Claude Berry was keenly associated with political work, and it was in Cornwall that he first met A.L. on the political stage. Pursuing his political career whilst on vacation from All Souls, the two had much in common. Their similar backgrounds a common link, the two became firm friends on their home territory. The new car, which A.L. had bought for his family about this time, was also used for Labour party business, which Claude and his wife would support. Claude headed the team of friends who supported Leslie's ideals on the rounds of political meetings within the County. He was sufficiently involved and enthusiastic to become the founder of a newspaper *The Cornish Labour News,* intended to further the Labour cause in Cornwall. A.L. was invited to become a main contributor. Published monthly, he was able to use it as a platform to air his hopes as a Labour candidate for Parliament.

A.L., in his turn encouraged Claude to further his own literary career and work towards editing *Cornwall* in the County books Series. It was eventually published in 1949 and in the foreword A.L. praised the edition for its authenticity by "The most distinguished journalist in the West Country." Claude Berry took the name of "Lef Camheyle" (Voice of the Camel) when he was made a Cornish Bard in 1950. A.L. was appointed "Lef A Gernow" (Voice of Cornwall) in the bardic roll of 1968, both appropriate for their literary lives.

Claude Berry died in 1966 and on the Padstow quay in 1972 A.L. unveiled the memorial tablet on the Claude Berry shelter, erected by local people in honour of a "Devoted son of Padstow."

Gorsedd in 1968 at St Just, when A. L. and Barbara Hepworth were made Bards
Photo by David Wills - St Just

John Betjeman 1906-1984

It was during his Oxford years that A.L. would have first met John Betjeman. As poets, the two men shared a similar world, A.L. declared that "JB really lived poetry," and with a profound appreciation of Cornwall an instant rapport. They also both loved church architecture and history, absorbing detail in Oxfordshire and Cornwall. John Betjeman's passion for churches was epitomised by an obsession with church bells, shared with A.L., and which featured in several of their individual poems. Inside a copy of *Summoned by Bells* in 1975 John had written, "To Leslie who has long been with affection and admiration of his fellow poet, John."

Born in 1906, just three years later than A.L., John Betjeman was in Oxford as an undergraduate during the mid-1920s. In a marginal note of the Oxford chapter in A.L.'s copy of *Summoned by Bells,* he had written with reference to the Botanical Gardens, "J.B. was first to take me there in a very old car." Describing Christ Church, John includes,

> "The place they call The House
> That shelters A.L. Rowse."

Interest in church architecture developed into a real and lasting obsession which they both shared. St. Endellion was one of their favourite churches in north Cornwall, often visited together especially during the Festival of Music held there each summer. A note inside A.L.'s copy of John's *Collected Poems* declared that John knew every City of London church before the pulling down of the 1930s and the destruction of the 1940s and could remember each interior with his extraordinary visual memory. Inside the copy of the same book, he had written, "My Prayer Book at Night," with special poems noted, "St. Cadoc," "Sunday Afternoon Services in St. Enodoc Church," "Greenaway" and "Trebetherick." Beside the last title he wrote, "My favourite of J's poems," and added that when invited to read it to the Royal Society of Literature after the Poet Laureate had died, he had been overcome with feeling at the loss of his friend. He also wrote, "I adore J.B's poetry, my feeling for it is like my feeling for Earl Grey tea - I can't get on without it. He's my drug. Also makes me cry." John and A.L. both possessed searching visual powers, constantly observing and noting people, places, pictures and conversations, placing every moment of experience on record. In his copy of *Uncollected Poems* by John Betjeman, A.L. wrote, "Oh, how I miss him! Life is poorer without him."

John had received a copy of *A Cornish Childhood* whilst in Ireland serving his country as U.K. representative to Eire in 1943. He reported back to A.L. of its success there and included his own warm praise. During the following years as both writers developed their interests they corresponded regularly. A.L. suggested unspoilt villages and ancient churches to visit in his native County, and added advice from his own experience of suitable publishers capable of reaching a larger audience. John was eventually to buy a home in Cornwall at Trebetherick, thus the two friends could often exchange visits. Some years later, when John was persuaded to compile the Shell guide to Cornwall, he thanked his friend A.L. Rowse, "who first opened my eyes to south Cornwall." Ten years later the two poets and authors compiled a Cornish book together. Published by B.T. Batsford Ltd, and entitled *Victorian and Edwardian Cornwall* from old photographs, the book combined Betjeman's attachment to that era in the choice of photography with A.L.'s scholarship as an historian.

Another interesting link between John Betjeman and A.L. was a mutual admiration of John Piper. A celebrated English artist, especially on architectural subjects, he had been a friend of Betjeman for many years. A.L. was introduced to Piper and was able to purchase a Cornish study of the artist's work, made during compilation of the Shell guide, a watercolour sketch of the mediaeval chapel at Hall Farm, Bodinnick beautifully outlined with Piper's fine lines etching the entrance arch.

Still corresponding regularly to each other in 1983, John would often sign his name, "Jan Trebetjeman," a pleasing joke between the two friends, referring to John's adopted Cornishness. A.L. appreciated and upheld John's views on contemporary society and twentieth century architecture.

When he died in 1984, A.L. received a bequest from John. It was a large

Victorian shell-work model of St. Mary's Parish Church, Penzance. Covered with hundreds of seashells and with interior lighting, it graced the entrance hall at Trenarren House throughout the remainder of A.L.'s lifetime.

Daphne Du Maurier 1907 - 1989

It was most likely through the Quiller-Couch family at Fowey that A.L. would have first heard mention of the Du Maurier family at "Ferryside," Bodinnick. Daphne, had once been entertained to tea in Jesus College, Cambridge with Sir Arthur Quiller-Couch, knew that his home was at Fowey and when her family moved there in 1927 made further acquaintance.

When the Du Maurier family moved back to London each autumn, Daphne did so with more and more reluctance, eventually persuading her parents to let her remain at Ferryside throughout the winter in order to pursue her writing career. She was befriended by the Quiller-Couches, with whose daughter Foy she had joined in expeditions to the Helford River and Jamaica Inn on Bodmin Moor, and was invited to The Haven for Sunday supper. This became a routine for Daphne when literary conversation predominated. When her first novel, *The Loving Spirit,* written at Ferryside, was published in 1931, Daphne admits in her autobiography that it was Sir Arthur's approval that counted most for her. The discovery of Menabilly, belonging to the Rashleigh family, and the fascination it held for Daphne du Maurier is well known and immortalised through her subsequent novels. Several years after her marriage to Major Browning, the family was able to lease Menabilly and lived there from 1943 to 1967.

A.L. had been introduced to Daphne by the Quiller-Couches, knowing that his historical scholarship and knowledge of Cornish matters would stimulate great conversation and empathy. A.L. advised Daphne which books to read while she was researching for *The King's General.* In a letter dated 1945, Daphne explained that she had had a lot of fun delving into the past, procuring reference books from friends, neighbours and libraries. She referred to help from the Rashleigh family (manuscripts and plans of Menabilly) and to the help that A.L. had offered by researching the Grenville family line in "Vivian's" pedigree. She quotes, "I have the bit between my teeth, am undaunted and determined to weave some grim tale of blood and intrigue out of these old walls." She concluded, "I do thank you so <u>very</u> much for putting me on these various books, and for letting me see Henderson's bequest. It was a true neighbourly and friendly act and makes a happy literary bond."

Kilmarth near Polkerris

From the section on the South Coast in *Victorian and Edwardian Cornwall,* A.L. refers to " 'Q', first of Cornish writers with his enchanting novels and stories and with a successor in Daphne du Maurier." A.L. and Daphne lived as neighbours across St. Austell Bay, but such was his tight schedule of work and frenetic travel, lecturing in America, with residence in California during the winter months, and periods at All Souls, that hurried visits to Trenarren left A.L. with little time for social visits. It was not until the 1970s, after the Browning family had taken up residence at Kilmarth, formerly the Rashleigh dower house, that A.L. and Daphne became regular correspondents and occasionally visited each other.

Daphne regarded A.L. as her, "Professor," as she was his "student," these words written inside the cover of *The Infernal World of Branwell Bronte* published in 1976 and which she had sent to Trenarren. Still researching and writing novels, Daphne acknowledged A.L.'s insight into the Tudor period, and always felt privileged to visit Trenarren for more conversation on the Elizabethan scene. She sought his advice on tracing Tudor characters, greatly admiring her contemporary still writing three or four books a year. In his turn, A.L. admired her research and triumph of fulfilment in work.

Occasional visits to Trenarren House to enjoy its garden in April, where

Daphne is remembered as a slight, trousered figure wearing a flat-topped captain's hat with a small peak, tailed off in the 1980s. However, Christmas cards and correspondence came regularly, A.L. referring to her as his fellow author living on the opposite side of St. Austell Bay. For both of them it is true to say that writing came first. A.L. claimed that Daphne was always natural with him, but on guard. When she died in 1989, he wrote in an obituary, "I

Daphne Du Maurier at Kilmarth

shall miss her, even though I didn't see much of her latterly. She was so shy and solitary, yet she was a world famous person."

David Treffry 1926 - 2000

Through his visits to Sir Arthur Quiller-Couch at Fowey, A.L. would have gleaned knowledge of Place and the history of the Treffry family who had lived there for seven hundred years. The charming mansion built on the banks of the river Fowey overlooked the magnificent harbour. The links of the Treffry family with the history of England and the port of Fowey would have captivated the budding historian.

A.L.'s initial visit to Place occurred during the summer of 1923, when at the end of his first year at Oxford and at home on vacation, he attended the County School swimming sports at Porthpean. Afterwards, being invited to tea with the governors and staff at Porthpean House, he was introduced to Henrietta Treffry. Discussion of Lewis Carroll and connection with Christ Church followed and A.L. was subsequently invited to tea at Place. "That historic house with its gathered towers and turrets," he records in *A Cornishman at Oxford*. He vastly enjoyed the interior and was presented with two of Lewis Carroll's books as a parting gift.

Ann Treffry, the next resident at Place and also a governor of the County School, would have been well informed of the success of the brilliant scholar and it is probably through this aunt that David Treffry first heard A.L.'s name. From a family who were avid readers and collectors of books it is almost certain that David would have been given a copy of *A Cornish Childhood* on publication in 1942.

It was most likely that A.L. did not meet David Treffry until the latter had finished his Army career in India and Pakistan, and returned to Oxford where he became an undergraduate at Magdalen in 1948. Further along the High, A.L. had been a resident Fellow of All Souls for more than twenty years and was well entrenched in his Oxford life. With the success of *Tudor Cornwall* and *A Cornish Childhood,* David and A.L. may have met through family connections in Cornwall. However, it is certain that the two Cornishmen, imbued with an intrinsic love of Cornwall, fine literature and verse, would have developed a strong bond of friendship at Oxford.

The friendship continued during vacations in Cornwall with visits to historic houses and villages. In a poem entitled *Native Sky* "For David Treffry", an awareness and affinity of the beauty of nature is shared. Composed during a visit to St. Mabyn, and sitting by the wayside cross there, five Cornish churches, all with saints' names, were visible.

> "The sleeping farms lie all around
> And never shall you or I
> Meet this magic moment again
> Under our native sky."

As well as forays into North Cornwall, a visit to Luxulyan in their own locality was always included and was a high spot of any vacation. A.L. and David would walk through Trethurgy, across moors and through lanes arriving at Luxulyan with time to explore the church and fine adjacent vicarage. On such a visit in 1948, A.L. describes the joy of its garden, "A dell of enchantment, lovely lawns with the screen of beeches and between the trees glimpses of the valley with its bracken-fronded slopes, boulders heaving up through the grass." On that occasion, they spent the afternoon walking along the leats, reminiscing of the days when the early miners had worked there. They passed under the Treffry viaduct, designed by one of David's ancestors, a fine silver-grey granite structure with ten arches spanning the valley and carrying the tramway and water for use in quarries and mines. Forty years later, the two friends spent Christmas day partaking of a pasty lunch under that same viaduct.

By the time A.L. began to further his career in America, David had joined the Overseas Civil Service in South Arabia. So correspondence became the main link, but in 1968, when David took up a post with the International Monetary Fund in Washington D.C, the two friends were able to meet on occasions in the United States. Later on, A.L.'s association with Lynchburg College, Virginia, provided a closer venue to Washington for frequent visits to David's home there. Letters and postcards were frequently exchanged.

In 1986, after David had retired to live at Place, succeeding his aunt, the friendship between the two became firmly established once more. By this time, A.L. had finished his work and travels in America and had settled back at Trenarren. Hospitality was often exchanged, many lunches were shared together as well as social gatherings connected with the National Trust and the Royal Institution of Cornwall, both causes dear to their hearts. They enjoyed the visits of mutual friends from all over the County and visited art galleries together. David attended A.L.'s poetry lectures and they shared the glories of Cornish spring gardens at Lanhydrock, Trelissick and Cotehele for several years.

In 1996, shortly after the stroke that so immobilised his friend, David also became gravely ill, but such was his foresight and determination, he maintained his watchful care over the household for his sick friend at Trenarren. David was the first to know of A.L.'s Companion of Honour award granted by the Queen in the 1997 New Year's Honours. He arranged a small celebratory party at Trenarren House on December 31st when the award was recognised publicly. Thirty of A.L.'s oldest friends met in the Library to share in the toast proposed by David. It was very moving to witness this great honour, being acknowledged and toasted by so courageous a friend whom A.L. had known for at least half a century.

David Treffry at Trenarren 31-12-96

David spearheaded arrangements for the Memorial Service in St. Austell Parish Church for A.L., after his death in October 1997, foregoing the one held in Oxford because of his own failing health. However, he was able to witness the unveiling of two memorials for his famous friend. One was the granite slab erected on the Blackhead in July 1999 and the second, a slate plaque, in Truro Cathedral in February 2000, both unveiled by Lady Mary Holborow, Lord Lieutenant of Cornwall. David died in April 2000, having survived his friend by two and a half years.

Spanning the twentieth century, there were few Cornish literary figures that A.L. did not know personally or by correspondence. These included J.C. Trewin, Anne Treneer, A.C. Todd, Geoffrey Grigson, Hamilton Jenkin, Jack Clemo, Charles Causley, Derek and Jean Tangye, L.V. Holdsworth the Quaker historian, Howard and Marion Spring and Winston Graham. He made it his business to know what was happening in the literary world, depending on his friends to keep him apace with new developments or trends. Of these, Raleigh Trevelyan, a descendent of G.M. Trevelyan (whom Leslie had known during his Oxford career) lived in Cornwall during part of the year and was A.L's confidante and link with current literary affairs. An author in his own right, Raleigh kept his friend Leslie informed about life in London and events at the Royal Society of Literature. A.L. now housebound in Cornwall still possessed an insatiable curiosity for literary and indeed world affairs.

A.L's many friends were from all classes of society, peers of the realm, country gentry, old Cornish families, bishops and clergy, scholars, educationists, publishers and loyal neighbours.

A. L. Rowse and David Treffry at the "Q" Memorial - Hall Walk

Chapter Eight

TRENARREN - THE LATER YEARS

A.L.'s years of research and lecturing outside his native county had made residence at Trenarren impossible for any long periods. However, during his visits home he soon settled back happily into a familiar comfortable routine with the members of his loyal "adopted family". He would ask for local news of people and places, relying especially on his two faithful and stalwart gardeners and friends Jack Blake and Jack Gill to keep him informed. Good neighbours and friends invited him to their homes for lunch, and in a congenial atmosphere, A.L. would bring them up to date with his world. He was a most entertaining guest with a store of witty anecdotes and amusing stories to suit any occasion.

In 1959 there came a chance for A.L. to show his appreciation and loyalty to St. Austell and the parish church in particular. It was here that he claimed his first aesthetic awareness of beautiful surroundings was aroused in the wonder of the stained glass and architecture. The parish church, Holy Trinity, was about to celebrate the seven hundredth anniversary of its dedication in 1259 by Bishop Bronescombe. To commemorate this occasion, A.L. agreed to write an historical account of St. Austell church, town and parish. In the preface, he gratefully acknowledged local friends and Oxford contemporaries who had supplied history sources and articles for his research. He concluded, "The time that I have been able to spend on the project is a very small return for all that I owe the Church."

The publishers, a local firm, handed over all the profits to the Church Restoration Fund. There were 719 subscribers to the first edition, priced at two guineas (£2.10) and produced in the spring of 1960. It was a fine edition, A.L. writing in an informative and interesting style, with excellent

ST. AUSTELL
Church, Town, Parish.

photographs provided by Charles Woolf of Newquay. There had been no comprehensive book written about St. Austell since the Canon Hammond edition of 1896, so this new one was well received.

A. L. receiving a buttonhole from Susan Fisher, the Vicar's daughter of St Peter's Church. Newlyn 1972

In 1972, A.L. took part in performing another public duty, an opening ceremony in the Morrab gardens, Penzance to mark the "At Home" of the Penzance library. The Morrab library, one of Penzance's distinguished institutions had been founded by a group of public-spirited townspeople. During the opening speech, A.L. praised the foresight of those people and referred nostalgically to the fact that it would have been a tremendous benefit to him from such a library in St. Austell in his boyhood.

In the same year A.L. involved himself in a more local matter close to his heart. He became the appeal fund patron for a spire and bells required for Charlestown church. He had fond associations with this church as his parents had been married there in 1893, forty two years after it had had been built in the newly formed parish of Charlestown. The tower had never been completed. The appeal fund was launched for £8000 and its patron, who had himself donated a thousand pounds, contacted many of his friends far and wide. John Betjeman replied immediately, praising his friend's appeal and sent him two autographed copies of his latest book for the fund raising process. Amongst others who replied to his letter was Noel Coward, whom A.L. knew had spent many boyhood summers in Charlestown and who loved the village, church and harbour. Noel generously donated £350, enough money to sponsor the light tenor, one of the six bells. It was called "Noel". *In A Cornishman Abroad*, A.L. recorded that when Noel Coward died a muffled peal had been rung.

St. Paul's Church, Charlestown

Diocese of Truro

SPIRE & BELLS APPEAL

£8,000 NEEDED

·CHARLESTOWN CHURCH· Proposed completion of Tower·

A.L. also wrote a new poem, to promote the appeal, entitled *Charlestown Church Bells*. An extract follows:

> Noel, Piran, Petroc
> Michael, Morwenna, Paul
> To the church above the harbour
> Sweet and silvery call."

He took this appeal to heart, not only because of his parents' marriage there but, because of his own appreciation of bells. Writing in his autobiography, *A Man of the Thirties,* he described the visual beauty from the rooms at All Souls along with the aural experiences. "Especially bells, which held a spell for me all my life," he wrote.

In his poetry, A.L. often refers to church bells and their meaning for him. In one, *New Year in Cornwall,* from his home in Trenarren he wrote:

"While over the shoulder of the hill
Strikes on the listening ear
From the navel of the parish
The last peal of the year."

Another poem, *Distant Surf,* evokes a winsome picture of the older man going up behind the back of the house at Trenarren and cupping his ear in his hand to try and hear the sound of the St. Austell church bells. He relates that although faint, he heard the "Distant surf of music on the breeze," and was consoled,

"To think that the church bells I remember,
From childhood can still be heard over the parish."

After the stroke, which he suffered in July 1996 A.L, back home at Trenarren in October, spent many hours alone with his thoughts. As the autumn continued he once asked Jack Gill to drive him to Oxford as he used to do. A.L. related exactly where they would stay there. "We'll go to Oxford, Jack," he would say. "You can drive us." Later still, towards Christmas, A.L. asked Jack more than once to take him to Truro to hear the cathedral bells. "Jack" he would say in his most imperious manner, which broached no argument, "I want you to take me to Truro. I want to hear the cathedral bells." Dear Jack used to comfort him, never refusing but instead referred to the inclement weather conditions, or encouraged A.L. to keep eating well to build up his strength again and then they could go. A.L. was always consoled, knowing that Jack would never let him down.

A.L. had retained a great interest of the Carlyon family at Tregrehan, stemming from his grandparents' role as lodge keepers there. He had researched the pedigree of the family and its historic roots. As secretary of the Tregrehan Mills Ladies' Group, I had written to A.L. in 1981 asking if he would consider coming to the village to give a talk about Tregrehan. It was a great pleasure to receive his acceptance and it was decided to make it available to all the village people. An audience of about thirty people was not disappointed. The great scholar was charming. He introduced to the village, that evening, a sparkling, historical account of earlier times, and with reference to the Carlyon family, he held us spell bound.

My mother, who attended, had brought two photographs of Leslie's mother in her days as a young servant girl at Tregrehan House, and handed down to her by her mother, head cook at Tregrehan at that time, along with other photos of the servants employed there. A.L. accepted the gift of these photographs and was greatly interested.

The success of this evening encouraged me some four years later after my mother's death to compile a village history, *A Village Portrait,* and to approach A.L. for a foreword. The very afternoon I called at Trenarren, he had been to tea at Tregrehan with Gillian Carlyon and was not at home. Phyllis Cundy, Leslie's housekeeper, who had accompanied him on his visit to the Ladies' Group meeting and had joined us at Tregrehan for subsequent Feast Day celebrations, agreed to show A.L. my proof copy, she thought, "When he is in a good mood." I realised the importance of this, knowing that it was a very "small" book compared with the academic history ones normally sent to him for review

Just as I was leaving, we heard the sound of a car. The black gates of Trenarren opened and A.L. saw Phyllis and myself inside.

"Who is this, Phyllis?" he said.
"It's Mrs. Brokenshire to see you," was the reply.
"What does she want?" staccato voice, impatient to get indoors.
Phyllis, knowing that all would be lost in seconds said, " She would like you to read her book," adding quickly, " It's about Tregrehan."
"Ah, then, when does she want it back?" said the great man. I cringed knowing the answer to come, the printer had given me a deadline.
"Tomorrow, sometime," said Phyllis.
"Help!" I thought. "This is it, he'll explode!" I was ready to pull the book from Phyllis and disappear. I held my breath, wasn't I invisible anyway? A.L. had not once looked in my direction.

"Tell her to leave it," he said and turned to open the garage door. "Go on, go on, quick," said Phyllis. "Come back tomorrow."

The following morning I called, and Phyllis met me at the back door. She was beaming. "He's done it," she said. "He read it, and wrote this before breakfast." She handed me the foreword, beautifully written on the back of a printed circular.

From 1985, relations between Tregonissey, where I lived, and Trenarren strengthened from year to year. A.L. bought several copies of *A Village Portrait* to send to his friends. Thanks to Phyllis, his housekeeper, I enjoyed visits there and became acquainted with the beautiful garden. When A.L. was in America, I would sometimes bring Phyllis back to Trenarren from her home at Pentewan to prepare for the great author's return and their renewal of residence.

On one such occasion in the spring of 1986, probably after A.L.'s last trans-Atlantic flight, which he detested, Phyllis and I were awaiting his return seated on the front terrace, drinking tea. The house was ready, the curtains back, windows open and provisions stored. Phyllis understood that one of the "Jacks" would have been contacted to meet the train at St. Austell station. All was peace and tranquillity.

We heard a car stop outside the gates, a scrunching of footsteps on the gravel and a loud, irate voice echoing in the drive. "Where is everybody? Why wasn't I met? Why was no one at the station?" There was A.L., struggling down the drive with brief case and luggage, our traveller in high old dudgeon. A taxi drove off at high speed!

"Where is Jack?" said Phyllis. "Didn't you let him know the time of the train?" We gazed at each other in bewilderment, but quickly realising A.L.'s extreme tiredness, his annoyance at not being met, combined with inner fury at his own omission, there was only one answer. "Tea," said Phyllis. "You go on up to bed."

Knowing of the two "Jacks" allegiance to A.L., I hesitated to interfere but trying to pour oil on troubled waters, I said, "If I had known Dr. Rowse, I would have been pleased to meet you."

"Then why didn't you?" he snapped. Reeling backwards towards the shrubbery, I tried to work that one out!

"Go on, go on," said Phyllis. "You go on up, leave your case in the hall. We'll bring up a pot of tea."

He shuffled away into the hall, stumped loudly on every stair tread with loud exhalations of annoyance on each one. We retired to the kitchen to make tea.

"You can't go on up yet," said Phyllis. "You must give him time to get into bed."

"Go up," I thought that was the last thing I wanted to do to face that alarming man again so soon.

However, after a suitable interval, Phyllis placed a tray in my hands to take up. "Call out 'you-hoo' outside his door," she said. "He's deaf, he won't hear you coming."

"You-hoo," I called twice outside the closed bedroom door, feeling more than a little alarmed about the angry bear I feared inside. No answer. Throwing discretion to the wind, I called once more, pushing the door open as I did so.

"Ahhh," a long contented sigh. "Thank you sweetie ~ you're most kind," from A.L., smiling most benignly from his bed. I placed the tray on the bed, he settled back to pour his tea. He was back home at Trenarren, all was right again with his world.

Jack Gill related that when he met A.L., after his American tours, at the station, Leslie would come towards him down the platform, his face beaming with pleasure. "Ah, Jack," he would say, "yours is the first, friendly face I've seen for days." Jack, a good friend since 1965, had always helped with the paperwork details of A.L.'s car, and spoke of his motoring incidents with some amusement. After leaving Porthpean Road, A.L. realised that he had to acquire a car and pass the driving test. Jack knew that he had learnt to drive in Oxford with a patient tutor whom A.L. claimed had vouched that among his pupils, he had only had one old lady who was worse! Taking the test at Bodmin, A.L. related to Jack a graphic account of it and the driving inspector whom he immediately engaged in bright conversation and then took the opportunity then to sally forth at his own convenience. Further into the test, A.L. was asked for a three-point turn in a narrow triangle. "Oh, no, no, no!" the inspector said as they came near an insurmountable wall, "That won't do, she can't do it." However, the car obliged by turning a complete circle. "I'd never have scraped," said A.L. "You know, you *almost* put me off." Jack would relate at this juncture that Leslie's eyes would twinkle. "All's fair in love and war, eh, Jack?" The inspector, bemused beyond belief, gave A.L. the pass certificate, but was further confounded when he wouldn't remove the L-plates and was told, "I want people to know who's coming." Jack never tired of relating this account. Was it the innocence or the audacity that fascinated?

A further story of Jack's relating to a motoring incident was even better. At Callington, where A.L. had parked by a 'No Waiting' sign, later claiming that he thought this applied only to buses, he was approached by a young policeman who seemed to be, as A.L. thought, taking a qualifying interest in his new car. "Your road fund licence?" he said. A.L. asked him what he meant. When told that it was the disc on his windscreen, A.L. had replied, "Oh, that round thing. I never knew what it was. I thought it was for my driving licence." The policeman apparently bemused, "It's out of date," he said. "How clever of you to know that. How on earth could you tell?" said A.L. There followed a moment of suspicious silence, then the policeman said, "There is a different colour for every year." "How fascinating," replied A.L. "I never knew that. You are obviously highly intelligent and destined to go far in your career. I shall see that your Chief Inspector knows. I am dining with him tonight."

"Then he drove off," said Jack," leaving a very confused constable in his wake."

Grateful for the foreword he had written for me, I offered support to the menage at Trenarren. Occasionally, I could help Phyllis in the kitchen. In the late 1980s, I helped with a lunch party for Sir William Golding, fellow author and a Nobel Prize winner, and his wife. Two other evening events about this time, when I served refreshments, were very pleasant social occasions. A.L. invited a number of his friends to view slides of Trenarren gardens, Oxford, Lanhydrock and Place, Fowey which had been taken by Jack Gill while visiting these places with A.L. The slides were projected on to the screen in the hall on the first occasion, Phyllis and I sitting on the stairs, and in the Library on the second. A.L. contributed a running commentary, liberally sprinkled with anecdotes of people and historical references on both occasions.

Social entertainment at Trenarren grew less into the next decade but A.L. was most agreeable to meet and encourage authors, literary friends, the press and other visitors at his bedside. During the morning, after he had dealt with the mail, or at 4 o'clock after his afternoon sleep, and supplied with a pot of his favourite Earl Grey tea, Leslie would regale his company with amusing stories, literary discussion or talk seriously on political issues.

During the winter of 1987, on one occasion while I was sitting at the foot of his bed, A.L. suggested that I wrote another book, about the history of St. Blazey. He told me to think about it, praised my first book, and then proceeded to dictate the titles of books I should read in order to get started. He made me promise to think about it. Such was his determination that he rarely forgot to mention the subject whenever we met. "Have you started St. Blazey yet?" he would invariably ask before dismissing me with, "Work, work, I must get on with *my* work." Once he looked up after one of my visits and remarked, "You should get on with St. Blazey," and with a twinkle in his eye, "I can't write *all* the books, you know."

One evening, after bringing Phyllis back to Trenarren after a family visit and going upstairs to see him, he commanded me to, "Sit down at the bottom of the bed." He gave me a small piece of paper and proceeding to read from *Lake's Parochial History* ordered me to make notes. Who could refuse such a man? He had patience to help me with further research but one had to learn that he dispensed abruptly with daily trivia. So I began to write, coming to many a halt as my full-time teaching commitments left only the holidays for detailed research. A.L. never omitted to ask how "the book" was progressing, and I realised that no one refused Dr. Rowse easily. When he gave me Peach's biography *Ralph Allen ~ Man of Bath* to take home and read, I knew then that I was committed.

Early in 1993, A.L. offered to read the proof copy. I waited anxiously for his opinion, this being a much more detailed study than my previous village one. He bade me to cut the book by a third. "It is too long," he said. "I am always having to cut my books. You should listen to me." His pen had cut through many paragraphs, comments were annotated in the margins, along with liberal sprinklings of exasperation. The proof copy had been brutally executed. Amending some paragraphs, and daringly eradicating some of A.L.'s obliterating lines, the text was somewhat reduced. A.L. wrote a foreword from memory and "St. Blazey" went to print. From that time onwards, I became his "author" and "local historian friend." He would give me one of his own books each Christmas and the following one he wrote inside the cover, "Valerie, many congratulations on her book and Good Luck with it, her friend Leslie."

A.L. was generous and kind, taking time to write a letter for me when he knew I wanted to visit Oxford. As an introduction to All Souls, what could have been better? "May I introduce Mrs. Brokenshire, a Cornish scholar to see the College interior?" That letter opened all doors. The porter to whom I presented it remembered Dr. Rowse very well. "We *all* knew him here," he said. I was able to visit the Chapel with its magnificent reredos, and golden winged angels set in the ceiling. By chance, it was All Souls Day, the lamps were still lit on the Fellows' places. A further visit to meet the librarian of the Codrington Library at All Souls resulted in a tour where one marvelled at the number of rare books and manuscripts. It was awe-inspiring. I felt the wonderful atmosphere of the place and returned to Cornwall with a better realisation of its importance in A.L.'s life. When I next met him, he was anxious to know what I thought of Oxford and All Souls. He listened intently until I came to the Chapel, then his eyes glazed over slightly, his head turned towards the window, as he remembered the many All Souls Day services he had attended. Time stood still, neither of us spoke. He was now ninety years old.

Local history was always a great talking point between us. A.L. kept in touch with Pentewan Old Cornwall Society and he had been a former member of the Society in St. Austell. One day, after mentioning the Domesday account of Cornwall, and that I had a friend who lived at Bodiggo, the manor of Bodwithgy in 1086, A.L. importuned me to take him there.

On a fine summer's afternoon, I drove him to Bodiggo. A.L. was terrified of the very narrow, winding lanes to get there. "Honk on every corner," he said, gripping his seat like grim death and keeping up a constant supply of caustic comments about any passing motorist. However, it proved to be a delightful visit. Eileen, its owner, showed him around the garden and the interior of the old house. A.L. studied the granite and slabbed entrance porch and the stone remains of the window from an early chapel, all the while enquiring about the field names.

At Bodiggo with Eileen Roach

On the same local history vein, I was able to show A.L. the menhir or longstone in a field at the top of Menear Road. He was pleased and amazed that on the many times he had walked up Menear Road on his way to Carn Grey, he had never seen the menhir, which had given the road its name.

Breage Church 1986

Further afield, and acting as his chauffeur, I took A.L. and Phyllis to Penzance for a book-shop visit, to check on stocks of *The Little Land of Cornwall* when it was just published. Returning home via Breage, A.L. directed that we stop by the church and taking us inside gave us a tour of its interior, wall murals and architecture providing a non-stop lecture on the church's history. As a patron of the Historic Churches Trust, he had headed the appeal for the preservation of the Breage wall paintings.

In the prologue to *A Cornishman Abroad,* A.L. describes summer in Cornwall at Trenarren. I wish I had known him in those days, for the two years I lived alongside the great man brought me a multitude of experiences, not least the delightful afternoon breaks on the terrace, above the challice-shaped lawn and beyond the Trenarren valley leading to the sea. It would have been another experience to have known him in former days when on his return from Oxford he joined forces with his two faithful Jacks to work alongside them and tame the garden. I only met him once when he was hoeing the border near the front gate in 1986. On entering the property and seeing him nearby, I called, "Good afternoon, Dr. Rowse." He looked up. "I've called to visit Phyllis." I added hastily, "How are you?"

"As you see me," was his reply and he returned to his hoeing with feverish momentum. There was no time to waste on niceties.

The two years at Trenarren from 1996-1998, when I was much involved with everything in the house, was a period in my life when I deem it a special honour to have worked for this great man. "This is your Oxford career," he told me one day. "I shall give you a tutorial. This is your literary career. Sit there!"

He was a man like none other I shall ever perchance meet on my journey through life. He impressed every one who came into contact with him by his personality and manner, his memory, superlative knowledge of world affairs, people he had met, places he had visited, book lore and history, all interspersed with a wry sense of humour. It was characteristic of A.L. to point out in the margin of his copy of *The Staniforth Diary* by Jean Hext that Sunday, October 4th 1800 was actually a Saturday! His vision of beauty surpassed that of anyone else I have ever known. The sunshine on the lawn was "Liquid gold spilling over from the Western sky."

There is never any doubt that A.L. completely loved Trenarren and knew that everyone else would too. The charm of the house won over everyone, the beautiful main rooms so tastefully furnished and the views of the garden were stunning. For most of his life at Trenarren, A.L. had jealously guarded its privacy, no one was ever welcome whom he had not invited but during my era he approved that I show his visitors or my friends his library.

I started work for A.L. Rowse in January 1996, after tiding him over the previous Christmas when Phyllis his housekeeper for nearly twenty years had been admitted to hospital. I helped organise the housekeeping at Trenarren and stayed there too on certain nights. I continued with Phyllis' routine exactly, blowing a referee's whistle at the foot of the stairs to let him know that breakfast was ready. A.L. would totter downstairs in pyjamas and dressing gown, take breakfast in the dining room before returning upstairs to work, reading and writing until the mail arrived. The same procedure occurred at lunchtime but this time he invited me to join him. He used to sit looking down over the garden and out to sea, regaling me from time to time with stories of Cornish friends.

In the New Year of 1996, when it became evident that Phyllis could not return to Trenarren to live, A.L.'s bed was brought downstairs to the front study, just inside the main door, where he claimed he would be able to hear the doorbell. He could also lock up easier at night. This suited him perfectly and he enjoyed breakfast in bed when I stayed overnight.

Looking in on him one morning before I retired to the kitchen, he said, "Did you sleep well?"
"Yes, thank you, very well," I replied.
"Everyone likes the air at Trenarren," he sighed.
Adding my appreciation of this I said, "I heard the birds singing early this morning.
"Yes, I slept well too." No comment about the birds!

It was agreed that I should come to Trenarren every day, on most days after breakfast which I had prepared the previous evening, organise lunch and share tea-time with him, staying overnight two or three times a week. The decision to become a housekeeper for him had not been an easy one to make. I had been visiting Phyllis on more than one occasion in the past, sitting with her by the small, antiquated two bar electric fire in her sitting room when A.L.'s voice would be heard approaching down the corridor.

"Coo-eee, Phyllis?"

Phyllis' walking stick would jerk forward immediately. "Quick, quick," she would say indicating the electric fire, "put out one bar. He's coming!"

A.L. and Phyllis both lived a spartan, frugal existence at Trenarren. She coped wonderfully with the whims and demands made on her. One winter's evening, when torrential rain had penetrated under the slates and was dripping through the ceiling into A.L.'s bedroom, Phyllis met me at the door, an empty ice cream carton in her hand with instructions to follow her to the attics to find the hole in the roof. I walked gingerly over the rafters, found the elusive leak and put the container in place under it. Coming down to A.L.'s bedroom, where a tin bath had been positioned directly under the ceiling to catch the drips, we reported on the situation. "Never mind," he said. "Put newspapers and cloths in the bath so that I cannot hear the sound. I can't work, otherwise." He continued with his writing, unperturbed.

I realised through Phyllis' accounts of various events that A.L. was an impatient man with little tolerance of human inadequacies. I also knew of other sides to his nature and treasure the letter of sympathy he sent me on the death of my father in 1991.

"Dearest Valerie,

Couldn't go to sleep last night for thinking of you. You are bound to be upset. Have a good cry, it is only natural. Then look forward to the future.

What is wonderful is that you helped to preserve him to nearly a hundred. To think that he was at school with my sister. That breaks a link for me.

It is a relief to think that there was no long illness and pain. Just dropping like a ripe fruit into sleep. That's the way we ought to go, painlessly.

When my father died, I immediately got a duodenal attack. So don't upset yourself and get it. Accept what comes to us. You have done your best. Now we must all stand together.

Love to you and the boys.
Yours ever
Leslie."

Another letter, again caring and compassionate, written after I had had a car accident on my way to Trenarren, made his case known. "I look forward to cups of tea with you here, while there's the library and all the books at your disposal." Persuasive words indeed. It still took much consideration before I consented to work for him.

As 1996 progressed from Spring into early Summer, life at Trenarren settled down into an even tenure. The garden surpassed itself. The camellias, flowering since the previous December, were followed by ranges of different coloured rhododendrons. The bank on the western fringes of the garden was covered in a succession of primroses, wild daffodils and later carpeted with bluebells. Though his eyesight was very poor, A.L. loved to hear news of the progress in the garden, and always approved of the arrangements that I brought inside. "Beau-u-u-tiful," he would say in his own inimitable tone. He continued to appreciate the natural beauty of the world, especially Trenarren from where now he never strayed. However, after lunch on the lovely warm sunny days, A.L. would ask, "Is it warm enough to go outside? We'll go outside together and sit on the terrace." I would retreat to the kitchen, A.L. would get out of bed, put on slippers and dressing gown, cross the hall calling, "Coo-eee," as he went. Placing his ancient Panama on his head, and selecting his favourite walking stick, we ventured out. A deep sigh of contentment would be heard as he lowered himself on to the seat. He would hold up his hands to the sun, turning them right and left. "Ah, feel the air," he would say. "Take deep breaths, fill your lungs with the lovely air at Trenarren."

Sometimes my six-year old grandson would be at Trenarren. A.L. enjoyed watching Oliver running up and down the front lawn on these visits. "Everybody likes Trenarren," he would say. "It's safe here for Oliver." I have a wonderful cameo etched in my memory from one of these occasions. A.L. had announced that he wanted to go and sit on the terrace and made his way to the porch. I held out his Panama hat, Oliver selected his favourite walking stick and we stood either side of the doorway. A.L. came from the lobby, turning to me took his hat then taking the proffered walking stick from Oliver, led the way, dressing gown flapping in the wind. The three of us filed in line to the seat, one behind the other. I glanced behind to see Oliver with his own imaginary walking stick, placing it fastidiously on the gravel, in perfect timing with that of A.L.

Still working in 1996 at the age of ninety-two, A.L. had just completed reading the proof copy of *My View of Shakespeare,* his latest book. He had also asked me to witness his signature on a contract for *Cornish Rhymes,* due in the autumn. One day after this he announced, "I am going to enjoy myself now. I shall read." He would ask me to fetch a certain title, telling me its precise location on a certain shelf of a bookcase. The book was invariably there! Once he asked me to fetch a book whose whereabouts he could not recall so well. "I'll give you 2p if you can find it," he said. Memorising the title and author, I searched in the library and eventually found it. "Take the 2p," A.L. insisted. "You've earned it!"

Throughout his life, A.L. had most stringent rules about the waste of electricity. Lights left burning unnecessarily in the house, electric fires of dubious vintage using two bars, were over the years like a red rag to a bull. One evening I had prepared his breakfast for him, the two eggs ready to boil, and left for home. The next morning A.L. found that I had left the main cooker panel switch down. A beautifully hand-written note was left propped on the mantelpiece. "ALWAYS put the cooker switch OFF." The fact that one might need the cooker clock was irrelevant. Twentieth century practicalities of life never impressed A.L.

Previous to beginning my time at Trenarren, I had booked a week's tour of Northern Cyprus. Thanks to loyal village friends and neighbours, A.L. was well cared for in my absence. The morning of my return, bringing him breakfast in bed, "Aaaah," he sighed. "Happy." He ordered me to sit on his bed later that morning while he related Lord Caradon's work as Governor General of Cyprus with marvellous recall.

We got on well together, life had returned to an even tenure for A.L. He greatly enjoyed visits from Phyllis and friends at teatime. When a friend of mine visited, A.L. wanted to meet her. We took tea together and he amused and instructed us with events in his life related to English aristocracy, famous society figures he had encountered at dinner parties and historical anecdotes. His conversation was charming, witty and compelling. We listened enthralled. We were his students and agreed that he was like someone with a light because everyone who came close to him was able to see more clearly.

After the stroke in July, which sadly immobilised A.L, Jack Gill and I kept Trenarren under close surveillance while he was in hospital. It was obvious that the uppermost and sole thought on his mind was a return to Trenarren House. David Treffry gave immeasurable support along with A.L.'s own G.P, Dr. Behennah, to engineer the undertaking. In October 1996, A.L. was brought back to his beloved home. The front study became his bedroom again. Jack Gill called in to see him.

"How are you A.L.?" he said.

"Ah, Jack, it's heaven," and smiling up at his loyal friend, "It's heaven." A pause. "Heaven to be back." It was a very poignant moment.

A routine was evolved to include resident twenty-four hour care. A.L. made some recovery, not in mobility but his appetite improved along with verbal wrestling with his carers. During that autumn, *My View of Shakespeare* was published and dedicated to H.R.H. the Prince of Wales. A.L. signed copies to send one to Prince Charles, friends in California and his loyal supporters.

Although bed-ridden, his presence was still at the helm at Trenarren. His lucid mind absorbed the daily manoeuvres around his care. "Any good post today?" he would enquire, referring to the many letters delivered each day. Several items would be read to him, and suitable replies composed for me to deal with. He was most exact. One day in conversation, he corrected my pronunciation of "really", in my Cornish inflection I had said "reely." "It's three syllables," he barked, "Re-al-y."

In November, we had a visit from William Waldegrave and Kenneth Rose, both well acquainted with A.L. through politics, All Souls and journalism. The three enjoyed lively debate together, A.L.'s asperity shining through as always. Preparing A.L. to meet the important visitors from London, Shirley, one of our main carers, leaned over to smooth his pillow before she left the room. "Thank you Valerie," said Leslie. "It's not Valerie, Dr. Rowse, it's Shirley." "Don't contradict me," came the staccato reply. There was still no doubt who was the master at Trenarren.

On December 3rd, A.L. celebrated his ninety-third birthday with a small afternoon tea party and his oldest friends. Although very frail, he was able to greet them all and later on nearer Christmas he said, "We'll have another party, like the one for my birthday." Celtic intuition, "deja-vu" who knows? In the 1997 New Year's Honours' List A.L. was appointed a Companion of Honour, a rare and distinguished award. This occasioned another party in celebration at Trenarren on December 31st. David Treffry proposed the toast to our great friend who had brought such an honour to Cornwall. This honour, conferred by the Queen, for A.L.'s outstanding service to history and literature, gave much cause for celebration in Cornwall that day. More than two hundred letters, including tele-messages arrived in the mail in the ensuing weeks. As reported in one national newspaper, "It completes his ascent from humble origins in a working class family."

From the House of Lords, and from their stately homes, some of the noble family names in Great Britain put pen to paper. The most distinguished of academics in this country, ardent fans in America, loyal friends from his Oxford life, and contemporaries who had followed his long career with pride sent many congratulations. Repeatedly the phrases: "Honoured to have known you;" "A mainspring and inspiration;" "Friendship and kindness;" "Encouragement over the years;" were written, along with: "Oxford and your college can bask in reflected glory." References were made to the Kings School, Canterbury, A.L.'s old mentor Quiller-Couch and his old County School headmaster. The honour gave much pleasure to his innumerable friends each recalling their own link with his life or career, and to many who only knew of him through his books. One signature was from "Cousin Jack, who has derived great pleasure and enlightenment from you and inspiration from your heroic struggle against adversity."

It was difficult to select which letters to read to A.L. He was not tremendously enthusiastic about them but an occasional smile would light up his face as he recognised names. After one particularly complimentary letter deeming A.L. "The greatest living Cornishman," the voice from the bed added sombrely, "half living."

In March 1997, Lady Mary Holborow, Lord Lieutenant of Cornwall, came to Trenarren to present the Companionate of Honour insignia of gold and blue enamel, surmounted by a gold crown, on a red ribbon and placed it around A.L.'s neck. It was accompanied by a scroll, signed by Her Majesty, "To our trusty and well-beloved Alfred Leslie Rowse Esq. Greetings." A.L. was in good form that morning. He inscribed a copy of his latest book for Lady Mary, adding his C.H. title. It was a truly memorable occasion. As we stood quietly in a semi-circle around A.L.'s bed, one sensed history being made.

In November 1995, there had been a first visit to Trenarren of H.R.H. Prince Charles, when he and A.L. had had a lengthy discussion on books and Shakespeare. A.L. recalled to me later, "I treated him like an undergraduate. He wants to come again." A year and a half later a date was arranged for another private and informal visit.

Arriving at Trenarren House by Range Rover, Prince Charles alighted, proceeded to enter the porch and, as I moved to greet him, said, "I've just come from Heligan, wonderful place. Have you been?" Having replied that I had and "Welcome back to Trenarren," Prince Charles made his own way to the Library where he knew A.L. would be waiting.

A.L. sat quietly in his chair, alas, far less communicative than on the previous visit. The C.H. insignia was brought forward, A.L. looked with interest as it was shown to Prince Charles but there was very little added to the conversation. He knew that a royal personage was present but this time age and infirmity had taken its toll.

Prince Charles left after three-quarters of an hour, pausing in the hall to enquire, "Who's Jack? Dr. Rowse thought I was you." This vastly amused Jack Gill standing nearby. Prince Charles enquired after Phyllis, remembering her from the previous visit and told us that he was distressed to see Leslie so different from the last occasion. Trying to make amends, I said,"Dr. Rowse so enjoyed your last visit here. His comment had been, 'He's like us, he loves books.' "
"Well, yes," admitted Prince Charles.

A.L.'s perception of human personality never ceased to amaze. In a book from Trenarren, which I had brought home to read one weekend, I found a poem written by A.L. entitled "Home." I read this aloud, not something I often do and tears came. When I told A.L. the next day, he always expected me to discuss the weekend's reading, that I had found and read the poem, he asked, "Did you read it aloud?"

"Yes," I replied.
"Good," he said. "That's how it should be." Then he paused, looked at me searchingly and asked, "Did you cry?" Then he moved on to say, "T.S. Eliot read wonderfully. I was second best."

Although A.L.'s infirmity was becoming more apparent, and he was sleeping for much longer periods, or seemingly sleeping, he was alert and aware of the life around him. He would break into a conversation with a correction of my pronunciation, especially the word "terrace" which seemed to annoy him. "You make it sound too long," he said more than once. "It's terrace, not terrraaace."
One day after another reminder about the same word, I ventured a mild retaliation. "I speak with a Cornish inflection. I did not go to Oxford University, Dr. Rowse. I only went to London for three years." "You should speak like me," he continued, ignoring the last remark. "You

should speak like I do." "If I spoke like you do, Dr. Rowse, my friends would say, 'Who does Valerie think she is speaking like that since she has been working for Dr. Rowse?'" "Bugger them," he exploded.

What a man!

Only once more did he refer to my Cornish inflection. When I was sitting by his bedside one afternoon, I noticed his mother's prayer book, which we had placed near him in the window. "Would you like me to sing a favourite hymn?" I asked. A.L. replied without hesitation, "Yes, 'Abide With Me'. It was Queen Victoria's favourite hymn." I sang two verses and noticing that he had closed his eyes for some while, I stopped. A voice from the bed pronounced, "You sing better than you speak."

During the last few weeks of his life, on arrival at Trenarren, I would visit his bedside. "Who is it?" he would say rarely bothering to open his eyes. "It's Valerie, come from Tregonissey."

"Good, I like it when Tregonissey people are around," he replied one Monday.

Dr. Rowse died very peacefully in his sleep on the evening of October 3rd 1997, as he would have wished, at Trenarren surrounded by his beloved books. A funeral service was held at Glynn Valley Crematorium, when his university silk hood and a Cornish flag draped the coffin, with flowers from all of us at Trenarren. The following week a final short service with the interment took place at Campdowns Cemetery, Charlestown.

In December 1997, on the day which A.L. would have reached ninety-four years of age, a Memorial service was held at Holy Trinity, St. Austell's Parish Church. Friends and representatives from all over Cornwall and Great Britain, reaching back over the years and spanning the last century, gathered to pay tribute. The Lord Lieutenant of Cornwall headed the dignitaries representing the County, London, Oxford, Cambridge and Exeter universities, authors, artists, clergy, historians were gathered there. A display of camellias from his garden were arranged to the left of the choir stalls which he had occupied as a choir boy more than eighty years before.

Christ keep the cliffs and coves,
  The land that gave me birth,
And let no harm come near to them
  When I am gone to earth.

Christ keep them as they were
  When I was but a boy:
To walk the roads and come to them
  Was all my summer's joy.

This was the land of my content,
  Blue sea and feathered sky,
Where, after years away, at last
  I came home to die.

Along the road a line of oaks
  Sturdy and strong were here,
Beside the deer park of Penrice -
  Now vanished like the deer.

I was young and head was high -
  Brave heart, do not despair -
For cliff and cove, headland and bay,
  Christ keep them as they were.

                                    A. L. Rowse

Poem read in St. Austell Parish Church at
Dr. Rowse's Memorial Service 4th December 1997

An Oxford Memorial Service took place in February 1998 in the chapel at All Souls. We travelled from Cornwall the previous day and took the opportunity to visit Christ Church, entering under Tom Tower as A.L. would have done seventy years before, viewed the Hall, Cathedral Meadows, and the great mediaeval kitchen. We tried to trace the footsteps of the young Cornish scholar thinking of his origins, his resilience and single-mindedness, which became his lode star.

Approaching All Souls along the High, the college flag flying at half mast over the tower at the entrance gate, we were presented to the Warden of All Souls, before taking lunch with him and the other special guests. The conversation centred around Cornwall, mainly of A.L as we knew him there but it was a moving tribute to be asked to offer a grace in the Cornish language. An Elizabethan recital, music, psalms, anthems and excerpts from Donne's poetry, was a part of the Memorial service. Facing the ranks of scholarly people across the floor of the chapel and listening to the address given by Richard Ollard, A.L.'s chosen biographer, I glimpsed a fraction of the significance of our great Cornishman, whom I had had the honour to know well in his last fifteen years. We realised that A.L. had known Oxford for more than fifty years. Before we left Oxford, we paid a last visit to the Codrington library and saw his signature in the Fellows' Admission book. It was the same as I had witnessed seventy years later at Trenarren, a fine, flowing no-nonsense style.

There were two other final public tributes to A.L. Rowse. The first was in July 1999, when an inscribed commemorative block of granite was erected on Black Head, almost within sight of Trenarren House. The second tribute was in February 2000, when there took place the dedication of a slate Memorial Plaque in Truro Cathedral. It was appropriate that the memorial was near that of his old friend Charles Henderson and not far away from the one for Arthur Quiller-Couch. The service of Evensong commemorated the life of A.L. Rowse, and included music chosen from the Tudor period, to reflect Leslie's lifelong interest in that age.

EPILOGUE

Early on in his life Leslie Rowse had been intuitively aware of uncommon capacities and had the greatest expectations of himself. He believed that the way to happiness was for everyone to fulfil their abilities as deeply and fully as possible. He was a prodigious worker, having written almost a hundred books, products of a first-class brain and phenomenal memory. Most of his working life was spent within the monastic decorum of All Souls, Oxford. A.L. read and researched avidly, enriching his initial perception of an actual moment in history to illuminate the past. Writing was his work and his life, his first priority. During the last ten years of his life he wrote fifteen more books.

Added to this amazing output spanning seventy years of the century was his capacity to appreciate visual beauty and spirit of a place, so finely portrayed in his poetry.

> "Inexpressible except at moments
> When the mind slips round a secret corner,
> Peers into the heart of an image."

Genius is intuitive and very hard to repress. Even in his ninetieth year A.L. would tap his head saying, "I have three more books in here." This life of the mind was incredible. It kept him on a single-minded course.

> "No, no ~ I'll not let go
> Until my last fruit
> Unfolds from the root
> And comes to bloom."

Most of us fortunate to have lived or worked alongside this legendary Cornishman, or shared his friendship, will treasure special memories. Seen by some people he met as self-opinionated, infuriating true eccentric with an innate touchiness to be avoided at all costs, those who really knew him to be generous, unmistakably engaging with an immense sense of fun, delightful and when he chose wonderful company, found him profoundly endearing.

What about the man whom I knew at Trenarren? He was a kind, amusing and entertaining presence in the house that he adored, surrounded by a beautiful garden and beloved library of books. He was a very sensitive and thought provoking man, though often seemingly brusque, impatient and certainly intolerant of people who did not use their time and energy wisely. He encouraged, inspired, indeed cajoled and badgered his younger writer friends to WORK. If I pause now I can still hear him going down the hall, after a little social visit to the kitchen saying loudly, "Work, work, I must get on with my work."

Cornwall was A.L.'s intellectual power-base and the centre of his affections. Gifted with a folk memory of its colourful past through study of his Tregonissey relatives and friends, he was proud to be Cornish, observing that as Celts the Cornish were extremely sensitive to character. I hope that this comforted him in his last months and weeks as those of his loyal Cornish friends visited, conversed or quietly sat by his side to the end. Maybe it was Celtic intuition, a strange pre-knowledge of things, but from a poem entitled Sunset, completed a few years before, A.L. wrote:

"Now when things have come right,
If late, yet not too late to enjoy
Friendly response from people
So long the object of mistrust;
Memories that crowd in from the past,
Friends that are dead and those
Younger who gave support
To my last days, giving warmth,
Happiness so long awaited
A radiant sunset glow."

A letter, I had written informing Duvall Y. Hecht, President and Chief Executive of Books-on-Tape in California, of A.L.'s stroke and return to Trenarren, received this reply, from which, with the writer's permission the following extract is quoted:

"I wept when I read your letter. Dr. Rowse has always been the very soul of encouragement to me in my work. Long before we met he glimmed our purpose and in his typically large minded and disinterested way, reached out with kindness.

I wonder how many other people he has touched this way. They are probably legion. I am proud to be numbered among them.

Please tell him that he has a very special place in my pantheon of heroes, and that for the rest of my life I will try to emulate his commitment to work, not forgetting to take time for kindness and generosity to others."

There are many people, who writing about Alfred Leslie Rowse would reveal another facet of his genius and personality. His mind had been trained and honed to a fine degree, absorbed by the life long work in which he excelled, to the exclusion of the many diversions life might offer.

In Cornwall, where only a certain permitted number of people knew him at all, he was held in high esteem, recognised for his brilliant mind and high ideals.

In his final two years, everyone who met A.L. for the first time could not help but be impressed by his still awesome presence and acute perceptions of his circumstances. He endeared himself to everyone, summoned to help at Trenarren. The words on a card written by a night-carer were a moving valediction.

"Dear Dr. Rowse,
Our meeting was brief, however enjoyable.
I kept you safe at night and you always knew
when I was there.
My warmest love,
Sarah.

Trenarren Garden in Spring

Trenarren Garden in Spring

Porch at Trenarren.
Overcoat and hats from the Oxford days

A corner of the downstairs study. In the upper section the lower four shelves hold a copy of each book written by A.L.

1987 A.L.R. Jack Gill and Phyllis Cundy

1987 Jack Blake and his wife Grace, with Phyllis centre.

Holding court.
A. L. in his eighties still working 1986-7

1987
At 5 Cannis Rd
with Minty, the cat.

Dr. Rowse
and the author
on his 88th birthday

Oliver Brokenshire awaits his Christmas book from Dr. Rowse 1995

June 1997 H.R.H. Prince Charles visits Trenarren

Memorial Stone on the Black Head

Oxford 7-2-98
Flag at half mast on
All Souls gate-tower
for the Memorial
Service of Dr. Rowse

ALFRED LESLIE
ROWSE C.H.
1903 — 1997
POET, HISTORIAN,
LOVER OF CORNWALL.

A. L. ROWSE
FROM HIS
FRIENDS

Campdowns Cemetery,
Charlestown

TRETHURGY

CARN GREY
ROCK

TO LUXULYAN

CARCLAZE
SCHOOL

TREGONISSEY

BIRTHPLACE
OF
A.L.R.

TREGREHAN
HOUSE AND
LODGE

COUNTY
SCHOOL

ROBARTES
PLACE

ST. AUSTELL
PARISH CHURCH
AND TOWN

A390

THE
LONGSTONE

CHARLESTOWN
CHURCH AND
CEMETERY

APPLETREE
MINE

ST. AUSTELL BY-PASS

POLMEAR
MINE

BRICK HILL

CHARLESTOWN

DUPORTH

PENRICE
HOUSE

PORTHPEAN

ST. AUSTELL
BAY

CASTLE
GOTHA

SILVERMINE

TREVISSICK

ROPEHAVEN

TRENARREN
HOUSE

MEMORIAL
STONE

BLACKHEAD